NIV
POCKET
GUIDE

R. A. Torrey

MarshallPickering
An Imprint of HarperCollins*Publishers*

First published in Great Britain in 1982
by Pickering & Inglis

Reprinted in 1991 by Marshall Pickering,
an imprint of HarperCollins Religious,
part of HarperCollins Publishers,
77–85 Fulham Palace Road, London W6 8JB

Printed and bound in Great Britain by
HarperCollins Manufacturing, Glasgow

CONDITIONS OF SALE

CONTENTS

Introduction

INTRODUCTION

This little book is prepared in response to a request from one who is, perhaps, in as good a position as anyone to know what Christian workers really want. It is not intended to supplant the larger work, *How to Bring Men to Christ*. Any who desire more definite and detailed instruction in the right use of the Scripture given in this book and in the general work of soul-winning are referred to the larger volume. Opinions of the most experienced workers may differ as to which are "the Best Texts" for any given case, but those quoted in this book are those which have approved themselves as such in the study and experience of the author.

There is medicine in the Bible for every sin-sick soul, but every soul does not need the same medicine. This book attempts to arrange the remedies according to the maladies.

PUBLISHER'S NOTE

This edition transcribes the Scripture passages selected by Dr. R. A. Torrey into the *New International Version* of the Bible. In addition, sections XII, XIII, and XIV have been composed and inserted to make *the NIV Pocket Guide* particularly helpful for dealing with significant problems of our time.

DR. R. A. TORREY

Dr. Torrey was regarded by multitudes during his lifetime as at the very top in soul-winning, Bible teaching, and the training of Christian workers. He was selected by D. L. Moody as the superintendent of Moody Bible Institute, where he established the Bible Institute curriculum and made Moody Institute a pattern for Bible institutes around the world. He was also pastor of Moody Memorial Church, Chicago. His courses on soul-winning and his practical methods stamped themselves on the lives of Christian workers by the thousands. Later he was the co-founder of the Bible Institute of Los Angeles, now Biola College. At the same time he was pastor of the great Church of the Open Door in Los Angeles.

But Dr. Torrey was primarily an evangelist. After the death of Moody, Dr. Torrey and Charles M. Alexander held the largest campaigns in America and then went around the world, winning hundreds of thousands of souls in great campaigns in Australia, New Zealand, and the British Isles, and on the mission fields of the Orient.

POCKET GUIDE

FOR CHRISTIAN WORKERS

IN THE NEW INTERNATIONAL VERSION

I. THE BEST TEXTS FOR THE CARELESS, IN-
DIFFERENT, AND ALL WHO DO NOT FEEL
DEEPLY THEIR NEED OF CHRIST

1. The fact and greatness of our sin.

This righteousness from God comes through
faith in Jesus Christ to all who believe. There is
no difference, for all have sinned and fall short of
the glory of God.   *Rom. 3:22-23*

If we claim to be without sin, we deceive ourselves and the truth is not in us. . . If we claim we
have not sinned, we make him out to be a liar and
his word has no place in our lives.
                                   1 John 1:8, 10

Jesus replied: "'Love the Lord your God with
all your heart and with all your soul and with all
your mind.' This is the first and greatest commandment."   *Matt. 22:37-38*

If you, O LORD, kept a record of sins, O Lord,
who could stand?   *Ps. 130:3*

2. The consequences of sin and unbelief

But the wicked are like the tossing sea, which
cannot rest, whose waves cast up mire and mud.
"There is no peace," says my God, "for the
wicked."   *Isa. 57:20-21*

Jesus replied, "I tell you the truth, everyone
who sins is a slave to sin."   *John 8:34*

All who rely on observing the law are under a
curse, for it is written: "Cursed is everyone who

does not continue to do everything written in the Book of the Law." *Gal. 3:10*

"Whoever believes in the Son has eternal life, but whoever rejects the Son will not see life, for God's wrath remains on him." *John 3:36*

And without faith it is impossible to please God, because anyone who comes to him must believe that he exists and that he rewards those who earnestly seek him. *Heb. 11:6*

"Whoever believes in him is not condemned, but whoever does not believe stands condemned already because he has not believed in the name of God's one and only Son." *John 3:18*

For the wages of sin is death, but the gift of God is eternal life in Christ Jesus our Lord.
Rom. 6:23

. . . And give relief to you who are troubled, and to us as well. This will happen when the Lord Jesus is revealed from heaven in blazing fire with his powerful angels. He will punish those who do not know God and do not obey the gospel of our Lord Jesus. They will be punished with everlasting destruction and shut out from the presence of the Lord and from the majesty of his power.
2 Thess. 1:7-9

"I told you that you would die in your sins; if you do not believe that I am [the one I claim to be], you will indeed die in your sins." *John 8:24*

Once more Jesus said to them, "I am going away, and you will look for me, and you will die in your sin. Where I go, you cannot come."
John 8:21

But the cowardly, the unbelieving, the vile, the murderers, the sexually immoral, those who practise magic arts, the idolaters and all liars—their place will be in the fiery lake of burning sulphur. This is the second death." *Rev. 21:8*

Anyone who rejected the law of Moses died without mercy on the testimony of two or three witnesses. How much more severely do you think a man deserves to be punished who has trampled the Son of God under foot, who has treated as an unholy thing the blood of the covenant that sanctified him, and who has insulted the Spirit of grace?
Heb. 10:28-29

3. God's love for us

"For God so loved the world that he gave his one and only Son, that whoever believes in him shall not perish but have eternal life."
John 3:16

You see, at just the right time, when we were still powerless, Christ died for the ungodly . . . But God demonstrates his own love for us in this: While we were still sinners, Christ died for us.
Rom. 5:6, 8

But he was pierced for our transgressions, he was crushed for our iniquities; the punishment that brought us peace was upon him, and by his wounds we are healed.
We all, like sheep, have gone astray, each of us has turned to his own way; and the LORD has laid on him the iniquity of us all.
Isa. 53:5, 6

And being in anguish, he prayed more earnestly, and his sweat was like drops of blood falling to the ground.
Luke 22:44

About the ninth hour Jesus cried out in a loud voice, *"Eloi, Eloi, lama sabachthani?"*—which means, "My God, my God, why have you forsaken me?"
Matt. 27:46

Christ redeemed us from the curse of the law by becoming a curse for us, for it is written: "Cursed is everyone who is hanged on a tree."
Gal. 3:13

11

For you know that it was not with perishable things such as silver or gold that you were redeemed from the empty way of life handed down to you from your forefathers, but with the precious blood of Christ, a lamb without blemish or defect. *1 Peter 1:18-19*

He himself bore our sins in his body on the tree, so that we might die to sins and live for righteousness; by his wounds you have been healed. *1 Peter 2:24*

II. THE BEST TEXTS FOR THOSE WHO WISH TO KNOW HOW TO BE SAVED.

1. Show them Jesus Christ as a Sin Bearer, the Saviour from the guilt of sin.

We all, like sheep, have gone astray, each of us has turned to his own way; and the LORD has laid on him the iniquity of us all. *Isa. 53:6*

He himself bore our sins in his body on the tree, so that we might die to sins and live for righteousness; by his wounds you have been healed. *1 Peter 2:24*

We are not like Moses, who would put a veil over his face to keep the Israelites from gazing at it while the radiance was fading away.
2 Cor. 3:13

This is love: not that we loved God, but that he loved us and sent his Son as an atoning sacrifice for our sins. *1 John 4:10*

He is the atoning sacrifice for our sins, and not only for ours but also for the sins of the whole world. *1 John 2:2*

For God was pleased to have all his fullness dwell in him, and through him to reconcile to himself all things, whether things on earth or

12

things in heaven, by making peace through his blood, shed on the cross.   *Col. 1:19-20*

In him we have redemption through his blood, the forgiveness of sins, in accordance with the riches of God's grace.   *Eph. 1:7*

You see, at just the right time, when we were still powerless, Christ died for the ungodly. Very rarely will anyone die for a righteous man, though for a good man someone might possibly dare to die. But God demonstrates his own love for us in this: While we were still sinners, Christ died for us. Since we have now been justified by his blood, how much more shall we be saved from God's wrath through him! For if, when we were God's enemies, we were reconciled to him through the death of his Son, how much more, having been reconciled, shall we be saved through his life! Not only is this so, but we also rejoice in God through our Lord Jesus Christ, through whom we have now received reconciliation.   *Rom. 5:6-11*

2. Show them Jesus Christ as a Risen Saviour, the Saviour from the power of sin.

Now, brothers, I want to remind you of the gospel I preached to you, which you received and on which you have taken your stand. By this gospel you are saved, if you hold firmly to the word I preached to you. Otherwise, you have believed in vain.

For what I received I passed on to you as of first importance: that Christ died for our sins according to the Scriptures, that he was buried, that he was raised on the third day according to the Scriptures.   *1 Cor. 15:1-4*

Then Jesus came to them and said, "All authority in heaven and on earth has been given to me . . . and teaching them to obey everything I have commanded you. And surely I will be with you always, to the very end of the age."
                    Matt. 28:18, 20

"She will give birth to a son, and you are to give him the name Jesus, because he will save his people from their sins." *Matt. 1:21*

Now if I do what I do not want to do, it is no longer I who do it, but it is sin living in me that does it.

So I find this law at work: When I want to do good, evil is right there with me . . . but I see another law at work in the members of my body, waging war against the law of my mind and making me a prisoner of the law of sin at work within my members. What a wretched man I am! Who will rescue me from this body of death? Thanks be to God—through Jesus Christ our Lord!
Rom. 7:20, 21, 23-25

To him who is able to keep you from falling and to present you before his glorious presence without fault and with great joy—to the only God our Saviour be glory, majesty, power and authority, through Jesus Christ our Lord, before all ages, now and for evermore! Amen. *Jude 24-25*

So do not fear, for I am with you; do not be dismayed, for I am your God.

I will strengthen you and help you; I will uphold you with my righteous right hand. . . .

For I am the LORD, your God, who takes hold of your right hand and says to you, Do not fear; I will help you. *Isa. 41:10, 13*

. . .Who through faith are shielded by God's power until the coming of the salvation that is ready to be revealed in the last time.
1 Peter 1:5

I can do everything through him who gives me strength. *Phil. 4:13*

3. Show them Jesus Christ as an Everliving Intercessor.

My dear children, I write this to you so that you will not sin. But if anybody does sin, we have

14

one who speaks to the Father in our defence—
Jesus Christ, the Righteous One.   *1 John 2:1*

Who is he that condemns? Christ Jesus, who
died—more than that, who was raised to life—is
at the right hand of God and is also interceding for
us.   *Rom. 8:34*

Therefore he is able to save completely those
who come to God through him, because he always lives to intercede for them.   *Heb. 7:25*

4. Show them that all they have to do to make
this Saviour and Everliving Intercessor *their*
Saviour from guilt of sin and from the power of
sin, and *their* Everliving Intercessor is just to
receive him or believe on him as such and confess him before the world.

Yet to all who received him, to those who believed in his name, he gave the right to become
children of God.   *John 1:12*

They replied, "Believe in the Lord Jesus, and
you will be saved—you and your household."
                                         Acts 16:31

"For God so loved the world that he gave his
one and only Son, that whoever believes in him
shall not perish but have eternal life."
                                          John 3:16

Declare what is to be, present it—let them
take counsel together.
Who foretold this long ago, who declared it
from the distant past?
Was it not I, the LORD? And there is no God
apart from me, a righteous God and a Saviour;
there is none but me.
"Turn to me and be saved, all you ends of the
earth; for I am God, and there is no other."
                                       Isa. 45:21-22

That if you confess with your mouth, "Jesus is
Lord," and believe in your heart that God raised

15

him from the dead, you will be saved. For it is with your heart that you believe and are justified, and it is with your mouth that you confess and are saved.   *Rom. 10:9-10*

"Whoever believes in the Son has eternal life, but whoever rejects the Son will not see life, for God's wrath remains on him."   *John 3:36*

"All the prophets testify about him that everyone who believes in him receives forgiveness of sins through his name."   *Acts 10:43*

Through him everyone who believes is justified from everything you could not be justified from by the law of Moses.   *Acts 13:39*

III. THE BEST TEXTS FOR THOSE WHO HAVE DIFFICULTIES

1. "I am too great a sinner."

Here is a trustworthy saying that deserves full acceptance: Christ Jesus came into the world to save sinners—of whom I am the worst.
                                            1 Tim. 1:15

You see, at just the right time, when we were still powerless, Christ died for the ungodly. . . . But God demonstrates his own love for us in this: While we were still sinners, Christ died for us.
                                            Rom. 5:6, 8

"Come now, let us reason together," says the LORD.
"Though your sins are like scarlet, they shall be as white as snow; though they are red as crimson, they shall be like wool."   *Isa. 1:18*

"For God so loved the world that he gave his one and only Son, that whoever believes in him shall not perish but have eternal life."
                                            John 3:16

16

"All the prophets testify about him that everyone who believes in him receives forgiveness of sins through his name." *Acts 10:43*

"For the Son of Man came to seek and to save what was lost." *Luke 19:10*

"All that the Father gives me will come to me, and whoever comes to me I will never drive away." *John 6:37*

2. "My heart is too hard."

"I will give you a new heart and put a new spirit in you; I will remove from you your heart of stone and give you a heart of flesh. And I will put my Spirit in you and move you to follow my decrees and be careful to keep my laws." *Ezek. 36:26-27*

3. "I must become better before I become a Christian."

On hearing this, Jesus said, "It is not the healthy who need a doctor, but the sick. But go and learn what this means: 'I desire mercy, not sacrifice.' For I have not come to call the righteous, but sinners." *Matt. 9:12-13*

"'I will set out and go back to my father and say to him: Father, I have sinned against heaven and against you.' . . .So he got up and went to his father.

"But while he was still a long way off, his father saw him and was filled with compassion for him; he ran to his son, threw his arms around him and kissed him.

"The son said to him, 'Father, I have sinned against heaven and against you. I am no longer worthy to be called your son.'

"But the father said to his servants, 'Quick! Bring the best robe and put it on him. Put a ring on his finger and sandals on his feet. Bring the fatted calf and kill it. Let's have a feast and celebrate. For this son of mine was dead and is alive again; he was lost and is found.' So they began to celebrate." *Luke 15:18, 20-24*

"Two men went up to the temple to pray, one a Pharisee and the other a tax collector. The Pharisee stood up and prayed about himself; 'God, I thank you that I am not like all other men—robbers, evildoers, adulterers—or even like this tax collector. I fast twice a week and give a tenth of all I get.'

"But the tax collector stood at a distance. He would not even look up to heaven, but beat his breast and said, 'God, have mercy on me, a sinner.'

"I tell you that this man, rather than the other, went home justified before God. For everyone who exalts himself will be humbled, and he who humbles himself will be exalted." *Luke 18:10-14*

"I have swept away your offences like a cloud, your sins like the morning mist.

"Return to me, for I have redeemed you." *Isa. 44:22*

4. "I am afraid I can't hold out"; or, "I am afraid I shall fail, if I try."

"I give them eternal life, and they shall never perish; no-one can snatch them out of my hand. My Father, who has given them to me, is greater than all; no-one can snatch them out of my Father's hand." *John 10:28-29*

So do not fear, for I am with you; do not be dismayed, for I am your God. I will strengthen you and help you; I will uphold you with my righteous right hand. . . .
For I am the LORD, your God, who takes hold of your right hand and says to you, Do not fear; I will help you. *Isa. 41:10, 13*

18

. . .Who through faith are shielded by God's power until the coming of the salvation that is ready to be revealed in the last time.

1 Peter 1:5

That is why I am suffering as I am. Yet I am not ashamed, because I know whom I have believed, and am convinced that he is able to guard what I have entrusted to him for that day.

2 Tim. 1:12

To him who is able to keep you from falling and to present you before his glorious presence without fault and with great joy—to the only God our Saviour be glory, majesty, power and authority, through Jesus Christ our Lord, before all ages, now and for evermore! Amen. *Jude 24-25*

"Be strong and courageous. Do not be afraid or discouraged because of the king of Assyria and the vast army with him, for there is a greater power with us than with him. With him is only the arm of flesh, but with us is the LORD our God to help us fight our battles." And the people gained confidence from what Hezekiah the king of Judah said. *2 Chron. 32:7-8*

But the Lord is faithful, and he will strengthen and protect you from the evil one.

2 Thess. 3:3

Who are you to judge someone else's servant? To his own master he stands or falls. And he will stand, for the Lord is able to make him stand.

Rom. 14:4

No temptation has seized you except what is common to man. And God is faithful; he will not let you be tempted beyond what you can bear. But when you are tempted, he will also provide a way out so that you can stand up under it.

1 Cor. 10:13

5. "But I am so weak."

But he said to me, "My grace is sufficient for you, for my power is made perfect in weakness." Therefore I will boast all the more gladly about my weaknesses, so that Christ's power may rest on me. That is why, for Christ's sake, I delight in weaknesses, in insults, in hardships, in persecutions, in difficulties. For when I am weak, then I am strong.   *2 Cor. 12:9-10*

I can do everything through him who gives me strength.   *Phil. 4:13*

No temptation has seized you except what is common to man. And God is faithful; he will not let you be tempted beyond what you can bear. But when you are tempted, he will also provide a way out so that you can stand up under it.
                                                            1 Cor. 10:13

6. "I have tried before and failed."

"Simon, Simon, Satan has asked to sift you as wheat. But I have prayed for you, Simon, that your faith may not fail. And when you have turned back, strengthen your brothers."
                                                        Luke 22:31-32

For what the law was powerless to do in that it was weakened by the sinful nature, God did by sending his own Son in the likeness of sinful man to be a sin offering. And so he condemned sin in sinful man, in order that the righteous requirements of the law might be fully met in us, who do not live according to the sinful nature but according to the Spirit.   *Rom. 8:3-4*

He gives strength to the weary and increases the power of the weak.

Even youths grow tired and weary, and young men stumble and fall; but those who hope in the LORD will renew their strength.

They will soar on wings like eagles; they will

run and not grow weary, they will walk and not be faint. *Isa. 40:29-31*

I have hidden your word in my heart that I might not sin against you. *Ps. 119:11*

For everyone born of God has overcome the world. This is the victory that has overcome the world, even our faith. *1 John 5:4*

Humble yourselves, therefore, under God's mighty hand, that he may lift you up in due time. Cast all your anxiety on him because he cares for you.
Be self-controlled and alert, Your enemy the devil prowls around like a roaring lion looking for someone to devour. Resist him, standing firm in the faith, because you know that your brothers throughout the world are undergoing the same kind of sufferings.
And the God of all grace, who called you to his eternal glory in Christ, after you have suffered a little while, will himself restore you and make you strong, firm and steadfast. *1 Peter 5:6-10*

7. "I can't give up my evil ways."

a. You must.

Do not be deceived: God cannot be mocked. A man reaps what he sows. The one who sows to please his sinful nature, from that nature will reap destruction; the one who sows to please the Spirit, from the Spirit will reap eternal life.
Gal. 6:7-8

b. You can.

I can do everything through him who gives me strength. *Phil. 4:13*

"So if the Son sets you free, you will be free indeed." *John 8:36*

Now, brothers, I want to remind you of the gospel I preached to you, which you received and

21

on which you have taken your stand. By this gospel you are saved, if you hold firmly to the word I preached to you. Otherwise, you have believed in vain.

For what I received I passed on to you as of first importance: that Christ died for our sins according to the Scriptures, that he was buried, that he was raised on the third day according to the Scriptures.
1 Cor. 15:1-4

8. "I will be persecuted if I become a Christian."

In fact, everyone who wants to live a godly life in Christ Jesus will be persecuted.
2 Tim. 3:12

"Blessed are those who are persecuted because of righteousness, for theirs is the kingdom of heaven.

"Blessed are you when people insult you, persecute you and falsely say all kinds of evil against you because of me. Rejoice and be glad, because great is your reward in heaven, for in the same way they persecuted the prophets who were before you."
Matt. 5:10-12

"For whoever wants to save his life will lose it, but whoever loses his life for me and for the gospel will save it. . . .

"If anyone is ashamed of me and my words in this adulterous and sinful generation, the Son of Man will be ashamed of him when he comes in his Father's glory with the holy angels."
Mark 8:35, 38

I consider that our present sufferings are not worth comparing with the glory that will be revealed in us.
Rom. 8:18

. . .strengthening the disciples and encouraging them to remain true to the faith. "We must go through many hardships to enter the kingdom of God," they said.
Acts 14:22

His speech persuaded them. They called the apostles in and had them flogged. Then they ordered them not to speak in the name of Jesus, and let them go.

The apostles left the Sanhedrin, rejoicing because they had been counted worthy of suffering disgrace for the Name.   *Acts 5:40-41*

If we endure, we will also reign with him.
If we disown him, he will also disown us.
                                        2 Tim. 2:12

Let us fix our eyes on Jesus, the author and perfector of our faith, who for the joy set before him endured the cross, scorning its shame, and sat down at the right hand of the throne of God. Consider him who endured such opposition from sinful men, so that you will not grow weary and lose heart.   *Heb. 12:2-3*

But how is it to your credit if you receive a beating for doing wrong and endure it? But if you suffer for doing good and you endure it, this is commendable before God. To this you were called, because Christ suffered for you, leaving you an example, that you should follow in his steps.   *1 Peter 2:20-21*

9. "It will hurt my business,"; or "I will lose my position."

What good is it for a man to gain the whole world, yet forfeit his soul?   *Mark 8:36*

"But seek first his kingdom and his righteousness, and all these things will be given to you as well."   *Matt. 6:33*

10. "There is too much to give up."

What good is it for a man to gain the whole world, yet forfeit his soul?   *Mark 8:36*

For the LORD God is a sun and shield; the LORD bestows favour and honour; no good thing

23

does he withhold from those whose walk is blameless.   *Ps. 84:11*

He who did not spare his own Son, but gave him up for us all—how will he not also, along with him, graciously give us all things?

Rom. 8:32

Do not love the world or anything in the world. If anyone loves the world, the love of the Father is not in him. For everything in the world—the cravings of sinful man, the lust of his eyes and the boasting of what he has and does—comes not from the Father but from the world. The world and its desires pass away, but the man who does the will of God lives for ever.   *1 John 2:15-17*

By faith Moses, when he had grown up, refused to be known as the son of Pharaoh's daughter. He chose to be ill-treated along with the people of God rather than to enjoy the pleasures of sin for a short time. He regarded disgrace for the sake of Christ as of greater value than the treasures of Egypt, because he was looking ahead to his reward.   *Heb. 11:24-26*

And he told them this parable: "The ground of a certain rich man produced a good crop. He thought to himself, 'What shall I do? I have no place to store my crops.'

"Then he said, 'This is what I'll do. I will tear down my barns and build bigger ones, and there I will store all my grain and my goods. And I'll say to myself, "You have plenty of good things laid up for many years. Take life easy; eat, drink and be merry."'

"But God said to him, 'You fool! This very night your life will be demanded from you. Then who will get what you have prepared for yourself?'

"This is how it will be with anyone who stores up things for himself but is not rich towards God."   *Luke 12:16-21*

But whatever was to my profit I now consider loss for the sake of Christ. What is more, I consider everything a loss compared to the surpassing greatness of knowing Christ Jesus my Lord, for whose sake I have lost all things. I consider them rubbish, that I may gain Christ.

Phil. 3:7-8

11. "The Christian life is too hard."

"For my yoke is easy and my burden is light."
Matt. 11:30

Her ways are pleasant ways, and all her paths are peace. *Prov. 3:17*

Good understanding wins favour, but the way of the unfaithful is hard. *Prov. 13:15*

12. "I am afraid of ridicule."

Fear of man will prove to be a snare, but whoever trusts in the LORD is kept safe.

Prov. 29:25

"If anyone is ashamed of me and my words in this adulterous and sinful generation, the Son of Man will be ashamed of him when he comes in his Father's glory with the holy angels."

Mark 8:38

13. "I will lose my companions."

He who walks with the wise grows wise, but a companion of fools suffers harm. *Prov. 13:20*

Blessed is the man who does not walk in the counsel of the wicked or stand in the way of sinners or sit in the seat of mockers.
But his delight is in the law of the LORD, and on his law he meditates day and night. *Ps. 1:1-2*

We proclaim to you what we have seen and heard, so that you also may have fellowship with us. And our fellowship is with the Father and with his Son, Jesus Christ. *1 John 1:3*

You adulterous people, don't you know that friendship with the world is hatred towards God?

James 4:4

14. "I have no feeling."

What feeling do you expect?

a. "The joy that Christians talk of"

But the fruit of the Spirit is love, joy, peace, patience, kindness, goodness, faithfulness . . .

Gal. 5:22

"We are witnesses of these things, and so is the Holy Spirit, whom God has given to those who obey him."
Acts 5:32

Though you have not seen him, you love him; and even though you do not see him now, you believe in him and are filled with an inexpressible and glorious joy.
1 Peter 1:8

"Whoever acknowledges me before men, I will also acknowledge him before my Father in heaven."
Matt. 10:32

And you also were included in Christ when you heard the word of truth, the gospel of your salvation. Having believed, you were marked in him with a seal, the promised Holy Spirit.
Eph. 1:13

For it is with your heart that you believe and are justified, and it is with your mouth that you confess and are saved.
Rom. 10:10

b. "Sorrow for sin"

1. Use passages for the careless, page 9.
2. Show that it is not feeling sorry for sin, but turning away from sin and receiving Christ that God demands.

Let the wicked forsake his way and the evil man his thoughts.

26

Let him turn to the LORD, and he will have mercy on him, and to our God, for he will freely pardon. *Isa. 55:7*

Yet to all who received him, to those who believed in his name, he gave the right to become children of God. *John 1:12*

They replied, "Believe in the Lord Jesus, and you will be saved—you and your household."

Acts 16:31

15. "I have been seeking Christ, but cannot find Him."

You will seek me and find me when you seek me with all your heart. *Jer. 29:13*

Then Jesus told them this parable: "Suppose one of you has a hundred sheep and loses one of them. Does he not leave the ninety-nine in the open country and go after the lost sheep until he finds it? And when he finds it, he joyfully puts it on his shoulders and goes home. Then he calls his friends and neighbours together and says, 'Rejoice with me; I have found my lost sheep.' I tell you that in the same way there is more rejoicing in heaven over one sinner who repents than over ninety-nine righteous persons who do not need to repent.

Or suppose a woman has ten silver coins and loses one. Does she not light a lamp, sweep the house and search carefully until she finds it? And when she finds it, she calls her friends and neighbours together and says, 'Rejoice with me; I have found my lost coin.' In the same way, I tell you, there is rejoicing in the presence of the angels of God over one sinner who repents."

Luke 15:3-10

"For the Son of Man came to seek and to save what was lost." *Luke 19:10*

All passages under II, page 12.

27

16. "I have sinned away the day of grace"; or "God won't receive me."

"All that the Father gives me will come to me, and whoever comes to me I will never drive away."   *John 6:37*

"Everyone who calls on the name of the Lord will be saved."   *Rom. 10:13*

Manasseh was twelve years old when he became king, and he reigned in Jerusalem fifty-five years. He did evil in the eyes of the LORD, following the detestable practices of the nations the LORD had driven out before the Israelites. He rebuilt the high places his father Hezekiah had demolished; he also erected altars to the Baals and made Asherah poles. He bowed down to all the starry hosts and worshipped them. He built altars in the temple of the LORD, of which the LORD had said, "My Name will remain in Jerusalem for ever." In both courts of the temple of the LORD, he built altars to all the starry hosts. He sacrificed his sons in the fire in the Valley of Ben Hinnom, practised sorcery, divination and witchcraft, and consulted mediums and spiritists. He did much evil in the eyes of the LORD, provoking him to anger.

He took the carved image he had made and put it in God's temple, of which God had said to David and to his son Solomon, "In this temple and in Jerusalem, which I have chosen out of all the tribes of Israel, I will put my Name for ever. I will not again make the feet of the Israelites leave the land I assigned to your forefathers, if only they will be careful to do everything I commanded them concerning all the laws, decrees and ordinances given through Moses." But Manasseh led Judah and the people of Jerusalem astray, so that they did more evil than the nations the LORD had destroyed before the Israelites.

The LORD spoke to Manasseh and his people,

but they paid no attention. So the LORD brought against them the army commanders of the king of Assyria, who took Manasseh prisoner, put a hook in his nose, bound him with bronze shackles and took him to Babylon, In his distress he sought the favour of the LORD his God and humbled himself greatly before the God of his fathers. And when he prayed to him, the LORD was moved by his entreaty and listened to his plea; so he brought him back to Jerusalem and to his kingdom. Then Manasseh knew that the LORD is God.

2 Chron. 33:1-13

17. "I have committed the unpardonable sin."

Show just what the unpardonable sin is:

"And so I tell you, every sin and blasphemy will be forgiven men, but the blasphemy against the Spirit will not be forgiven. Anyone who speaks a word against the Son of Man will be forgiven, but anyone who speaks against the Holy Spirit will not be forgiven, either in this age or in the age to come." *Matt. 12:31-32*

Explain Heb. 6:4-6:

It is impossible for those who have once been enlightened, who have tasted the heavenly gift, who have shared in the Holy Spirit, who have tasted the goodness of the word of God and the powers of the coming age, if they fall away, to be brought back to repentance, because to their loss they are crucifying the Son of God all over again and subjecting him to public disgrace.

This describes one who "falls away," i.e., becomes an apostate, renounces Christianity, and goes back to Judaism; not one who merely falls into sin, even deep sin, as Peter did.

Then use passages under 16, pages 28-29.

18. "It is too late."

When you are in distress and all these things have happened to you, then in later days you will

29

return to the LORD your God and obey him. For the LORD your God is a merciful God; he will not abandon or destroy you or forget the covenant with your forefathers, which he confirmed to them by oath.   *Deut. 4:30-31*

The Lord is not slow in keeping his promise, as some understand slowness. He is patient with you, not wanting anyone to perish, but everyone to come to repentance.   *2 Peter 3:9*

The Spirit and the bride say, "Come!" And let him who hears say, "Come!" Whoever is thirsty, let him come; and whoever wishes, let him take the free gift of the water of life.   *Rev. 22:17*

19. "Christians are so inconsistent."

So then, each of us will give an account of himself to God.   *Rom. 14:12*

You, therefore, have no excuse, you who pass judgment on someone else, for at whatever point you judge the other, you are condemning yourself, because you who pass judgment do the same things. Now we know that God's judgment against those who do such things is based on truth. So when you, a mere man, pass judgment on them and yet do the same things, do you think you will escape God's judgment? Or do you show contempt for the riches of his kindness, tolerance and patience, not realising that God's kindness leads you towards repentance?

But because of your stubbornness and your unrepentant heart, you are storing up wrath against yourself for the day of God's wrath, when his righteous judgment will be revealed.

Rom. 2:1-5

"Do not judge, or you too will be judged. For in the same way you judge others, you will be judged, and with the measure you use, it will be measured to you.

"Why do you look at the speck of sawdust in

your brother's eye and pay no attention to the plank in your own eye? How can you say to your brother, 'Let me take the speck out of your eye,' when all the time there is a plank in your own eye? You hypocrite, first take the plank out of your own eye, and then you will see clearly to remove the speck from your brother's eye."

Matt. 7:1-5

20. "God seems to me to be unjust and cruel."

But who are you, O man, to talk back to God? "Shall what is formed say to him who formed it, 'Why did you make me like this?'"

Rom. 9:20

Oh, the depth of the riches of the wisdom and knowledge of God!

How unsearchable his judgments, and his paths beyond tracing out!   *Rom. 11:33*

"For my thoughts are not your thoughts, neither are your ways my ways," declares the LORD.

"As the heavens are higher than the earth, so are my ways higher than your ways and my thoughts than your thoughts."   *Isa. 55:8-9*

"Will the one who contends with the Almighty correct him?

"Let him who accuses God answer him!"

Job 40:2

And you have forgotten that word of encouragement that addresses you as sons:

"My son, do not make light of the Lord's discipline, and do not lose heart when he rebukes you, because the Lord disciplines those whom he loves, and he punishes everyone he accepts as a son."

Endure hardship as discipline; God is treating you as sons. For what son is not disciplined by his father? . . . Our fathers disciplined us for a little while as they thought best; but God disciplines us for our good, that we may share in his holiness. No discipline seems pleasant at the time, but

31

painful. Later on, however, it produces a harvest of righteousness and peace for those who have been trained by it. *Heb. 12:5-7, 10-11*

21. "There are so many things in the Bible which I cannot understand."

The man without the Spirit does not accept the things that come from the Spirit of God, for they are foolishness to him and he cannot understand them, because they are spiritually discerned.
1 Cor. 2:14

Oh, the depth of the riches of the wisdom and knowledge of God!

How unsearchable his judgments, and his paths beyond tracing out! *Rom. 11:33*

When I was a child, I talked like a child, I thought like a child, I reasoned like a child. When I became a man, I put childish ways behind me. Now we see but a poor reflection; then we shall see face to face. Now I know in part; then I shall know fully, even as I am fully known.
1 Cor. 13:11-12

Open my eyes that I may see wonderful things in your law. *Ps. 119:18*

He writes the same way in all his letters, speaking in them of these matters. His letters contain some things that are hard to understand, which ignorant and unstable people distort, as they do the other Scriptures, to their own destruction.

Therefore, dear friends, since you already know this, be on your guard so that you may not be carried away by the error of lawless men and fall from your secure position. But grow in the grace and knowledge of our Lord and Saviour Jesus Christ. To him be glory both now and forever! Amen. *2 Peter 3:16-18*

22. "There is someone I can't forgive."

"But if you do not forgive men their sins, your Father will not forgive your sins." *Matt. 6:15*

"Therefore, the kingdom of heaven is like a king who wanted to settle accounts with his servants. As he began the settlement, a man who owed him ten thousand talents was brought to him. Since he was not able to pay, the master ordered that he and his wife and his children and all that he had be sold to repay the debt.

"The servant fell on his knees before him. 'Be patient with me,' he begged, 'and I will pay back everything.' The servant's master took pity on him, cancelled the debt and let him go.

"But when that servant went out, he found one of his fellow servants who owed him a hundred denarii. He grabbed him and began to choke him. 'Pay back what you owe me!' he demanded.

"His fellow servant fell to his knees and begged him, 'Be patient with me, and I will pay you back.'

"But he refused. Instead, he went off and had the man thrown into prison until he could pay the debt. When the other servants saw what had happened, they were greatly distressed and went and told their master everything that had happened.

"Then the master called the servant in. 'You wicked servant,' he said, 'I cancelled all that debt of yours because you begged me to. Shouldn't you have had mercy on your fellow servant just as I had on you?' In anger his master turned him over to the jailers until he should pay back all he owed.

"This is how my heavenly Father will treat each of you unless you forgive your brother from your heart." *Matt. 18:23-35*

Be kind and compassionate to one another, forgiving each other, just as in Christ God forgave you. *Eph. 4:32*

I can do everything through him who gives me strength.   *Phil. 4:13*

But the fruit of the Spirit is love, joy, peace, patience, kindness, goodness, faithfulness, gentleness and self-control. Against such things there is no law.   *Gal. 5:22-23*

IV. THE BEST TEXTS FOR THOSE WHO ENTERTAIN FALSE HOPES

1. The hope of being saved by a righteous life.

Know that a man is not justified by observing the law, but by faith in Jesus Christ. So we, too, have put our faith in Christ Jesus that we may be justified by faith in Christ and not by observing the law, because by observing the law no-one will be justified.   *Gal. 2:16*

Now we know that whatever the law says, it says to those who are under the law, so that every mouth may be silenced and the whole world held accountable to God. Therefore no-one will be declared righteous in his sight by observing the law; rather, through the law we become conscious of sin.   *Rom. 3:19-20*

All who rely on observing the law are under a curse, for it is written: "Cursed is everyone who does not continue to do everything written in the Book of the Law."   *Gal. 3:10*

Jesus replied: "'Love the Lord your God with all your heart and with all your soul and with all your mind.' This is the first and greatest commandment."   *Matt. 22:37-38*

For whoever keeps the whole law and yet stumbles at just one point is guilty of breaking all of it.   *James 2:10*

34

"For I tell you that unless your righteousness surpasses that of the Pharisees and the teachers of the law, you will certainly not enter the kingdom of heaven."   *Matt. 5:20*

"Two men went up to the temple to pray, one a Pharisee and the other a tax collector. The Pharisee stood up and prayed about himself: 'God, I thank you that I am not like all other men—robbers, evildoers, adulterers—or even like this tax collector. I fast twice a week and give a tenth of all I get.'

"But the tax collector stood at a distance. He would not even look up to heaven, but beat his breast and said, 'God, have mercy on me, a sinner.'

"I tell you that this man, rather than the other, went home justified before God. For everyone who exalts himself will be humbled, and he who humbles himself will be exalted."
                                                        Luke 18:10-14

He said to them, "You are the ones who justify yourselves in the eyes of men, but God knows your hearts. What is highly valued among men is detestable in God's sight."   *Luke 16:15*

This will take place on the day when God will judge men's secrets through Jesus Christ, as my gospel declares.   *Rom. 2:16*

But the LORD said to Samuel, "Do not consider his appearance or his height, for I have rejected him. The LORD does not look at the things man looks at. Man looks at the outward appearance, but the LORD looks at the heart."
                                                        1 Sam. 16:7

And without faith it is impossible to please God, because anyone who comes to him must believe that he exists and that he rewards those who earnestly seek him.   *Heb. 11:6*

Jesus answered, "The work of God is this: to believe in the one he has sent."   *John 6:29*

35

"Whoever believes in the Son has eternal life, but whoever rejects the Son will not see life, for God's wrath remains on him."   *John 3:36*

Anyone who rejected the law of Moses died without mercy on the testimony of two or three witnesses. How much more severely do you think a man deserves to be punished who has trampled the Son of God under foot, who has treated as an unholy thing the blood of the covenant that sanctified him, and who has insulted the Spirit of grace?   *Heb. 10:28-29*

2. The hope that "God is too good to damn anyone"

Or do you show contempt for the riches of his kindness, tolerance and patience, not realising that God's kindness leads you towards repentance? But because of your stubbornness and your unrepentant heart, you are storing up wrath against yourself for the day of God's wrath, when his righteous judgment will be revealed.

Rom. 2:4-5

Once more Jesus said to them, "I am going away, and you will look for me, and you will die in your sin. Where I go, you cannot come." . . . "I told you that you would die in your sins; if you do not believe that I am [the one I claim to be], you will indeed die in your sins."   *John 8:21, 24*

"Whoever believes in the Son has eternal life, but whoever rejects the Son will not see life, for God's wrath remains on him."   *John 3:36*

"Yet you refuse to come to me to have life."

John 5:40

The Lord is not slow in keeping his promise, as some understand slowness. He is patient with you, not wanting anyone to perish, but everyone to come to repentance.

But the day of the Lord will come like a thief.

The heavens will disappear with a roar; the elements will be destroyed by fire, and the earth and everything in it will be laid bare.

Since everything will be destroyed in this way, what kind of people ought you to be? You ought to live holy and godly lives.　　　*2 Peter 3:9-11*

"Say to them, 'As surely as I live, declares the Sovereign LORD, I take no pleasure in the death of the wicked, but rather that they turn from their ways and live. Turn! Turn from your evil ways! Why will you die, O house of Israel?'"
Ezek. 33:11

For if God did not spare angels when they sinned, but sent them to hell, putting them into gloomy dungeons to be held for judgment; if he did not spare the ancient world when he brought the flood on its ungodly people, but protected Noah, a preacher of righteousness, and seven others; if he condemned the cities of Sodom and Gomorrah by burning them to ashes, and made them an example of what is going to happen to the ungodly;—if this is so, then the Lord knows how to rescue godly men from trials and to hold the unrighteous for the day of judgment, while continuing their punishment.

2 Peter 2:4-6, 9

"I tell you, no! But unless you repent, you too will all perish."　　　*Luke 13:3*

"Whoever believes in him is not condemned, but whoever does not believe stands condemned already because he has not believed in the name of God's one and only Son."　　　*John 3:18*

But the wicked are like the tossing sea, which cannot rest, whose waves cast up mire and mud.
"There is no peace," says my God, "for the wicked."　　　*Isa. 57:20-21*

3. The hope of being saved by "trying to be a Christian"

It is not trying what we can do, but trusting what Jesus has done, and will do, that saves.

For all have sinned and fall short of the glory of God, and are justified freely by his grace through the redemption that came by Christ Jesus. God presented him as a sacrifice of atonement, through faith in his blood. He did this to demonstrate his justice, because in his forbearance he had left the sins committed beforehand unpunished. *Rom. 3:23-25*

What does the Scripture say? "Abraham believed God, and it was credited to him as righteousness."

Now when a man works, his wages are not credited to him as a gift, but as an obligation. However, to the man who does not work but trusts God who justifies the wicked, his faith is credited as righteousness. *Rom. 4:3-5*

To him who is able to keep you from falling and to present you before his glorious presence without fault and with great joy—to the only God our Saviour be glory, majesty, power and authority, through Jesus Christ our Lord, before all ages, now and for evermore! Amen. *Jude 24-25*

Yet to all who received him, to those who believed in his name, he gave the right to become children of God. *John 1:12*

They replied, "Believe in the Lord Jesus, and you will be saved—you and your household." *Acts 16:31*

That is why I am suffering as I am. Yet I am not ashamed, because I know whom I have believed, and am convinced that he is able to guard what I have entrusted to him for that day.

2 Tim. 1:12

Surely God is my salvation; I will trust and not be afraid.

The LORD, the LORD, is my strength and my song; he has become my salvation."   *Isa. 12:2*

4. The hope of being saved because "I feel saved," or "I feel that I am going to heaven"

Show that we should build our hope not on what we feel, but on what God says.

There is a way that seems right to a man, but in the end it leads to death.   *Prov. 14:12*

. . . a faith and knowledge resting on the hope of eternal life, which God, who does not lie, promised before the beginning of time.

Titus 1:2

"Whoever believes in the Son has eternal life, but whoever rejects the Son will not see life, for God's wrath remains on him."   *John 3:36*

To some who were confident of their own righteousness and looked down on everybody else, Jesus told this parable:

"Two men went up to the temple to pray, one a Pharisee and the other a tax collector. The Pharisee stood up and prayed about himself: 'God, I thank you that I am not like all other men—robbers, evildoers, adulterers—or even like this tax collector. I fast twice a week and give a tenth of all I get.'

"But the tax collector stood at a distance. He would not even look up to heaven, but beat his breast and said, 'God, have mercy on me, a sinner.'

"I tell you that this man, rather than the other, went home justified before God. For everyone who exalts himself will be humbled, and he who humbles himself will be exalted."

Luke 18:9-14

5. The hope of being saved by a profession, or church membership, or faith, that does not save us from sin

Make every effort to live in peace with all men and to be holy; without holiness no-one will see the Lord. *Heb. 12:14*

Do you not know that the wicked will not inherit the kingdom of God? Do not be deceived: Neither the sexually immoral nor idolaters nor adulterers nor male prostitutes nor homosexual offenders nor thieves nor the greedy nor drunkards nor slanderers nor swindlers will inherit the kingdom of God. *1 Cor. 6:9-10*

They claim to know God, but by their actions they deny him. They are detestable, disobedient and unfit for doing anything good. *Titus 1:16*

What good is it, my brothers, if a man claims to have faith but has no deeds? Can such faith save him? *James 2:14*

In reply Jesus declared, "I tell you the truth, unless a man is born again, he cannot see the kingdom of God." *John 3:3*

If you know that he is righteous, you know that everyone who does what is right has been born of him. *1 John 2:29*

For everyone born of God has overcome the world. This is the victory that has overcome the world, even our faith. Who is it that overcomes the world? Only he who believes that Jesus is the Son of God. *1 John 5:4-5*

"But the cowardly, the unbelieving, the vile, the murderers, the sexually immoral, those who practise magic arts, the idolaters and all liars—their place will be in the fiery lake of burning sulphur. This is the second death." *Rev. 21:8*

V. THE BEST TEXTS FOR THOSE WHO LACK ASSURANCE

I write these things to you who believe in the name of the Son of God so that you may know that you have eternal life. *1 John 5:13*

Yet to all who received him, to those who believed in his name, he gave the right to become children of God. *John 1:12*

"Whoever believes in the Son has eternal life, but whoever rejects the Son will not see life, for God's wrath remains on him." *John 3:36*

"I tell you the truth, whoever hears my word and believes him who sent me has eternal life and will not be condemned; he has crossed over from death to life." *John 5:24*

"Through him everyone who believes is justified from everything you could not be justified from by the law of Moses." *Acts 13:39*

And this is the testimony: God has given us eternal life, and this life is in his Son. He who has the Son has life; he who does not have the Son of God does not have life. *1 John 5:11-12*

When Jesus spoke again to the people, he said, "I am the light of the world. Whoever follows me will never walk in darkness, but will have the light of life." *John 8:12*

Let the wicked forsake his way and the evil man his thoughts.

Let him turn to the LORD, and he will have mercy on him, and to our God, for he will freely pardon. *Isa. 55:7*

VI. THE BEST TEXTS FOR BACKSLIDERS

1. Careless Backsliders

This is what the LORD says:

"What fault did your fathers find in me, that they strayed so far from me?

They followed worthless idols and became worthless themselves. . . .

"My people have committed two sins: They have forsaken me, the spring of living water, and have dug their own cisterns, broken cisterns that cannot hold water. . . .

"Your wickedness will punish you; your backsliding will rebuke you.

Consider then and realise how evil and bitter it is for you when you forsake the LORD your God and have no awe of me," declares the Lord, the LORD Almighty.   *Jer. 2:5, 13, 19*

"I overthrew some of you as I overthrew Sodom and Gomorrah.

You were like a burning stick snatched from the fire, yet you have not returned to me," declares the LORD.

"Therefore this is what I will do to you, Israel, and because I will do this to you, prepare to meet your God, O Israel."   *Amos 4:11-12*

The LORD became angry with Solomon because his heart had turned away from the LORD, the God of Israel, who had appeared to him twice.

1 Kings 11:9

The faithless will be fully repaid for their ways, and the good man rewarded for his.

Prov. 14:14

2. Backsliders who wish to come back to the Lord.

Go, proclaim this message towards the north:

" 'Return, faithless Israel,' declares the LORD, 'I will frown on you no longer, for I am merciful,' declares the LORD, 'I will not be angry for ever.

Only acknowledge your guilt—you have rebelled against the LORD your God, you have scattered your favours to foreign gods. . . .'

42

"Return, faithless people; I will cure you of backsliding."

"Yes, we will come to you, for you are the LORD our God." *Jer. 3:12-13, 22*

Return, O Israel, to the LORD your God. Your sins have been your downfall!

Take words with you and return to the LORD.

Say to him: "Forgive all our sins and receive us graciously, that we may offer the fruit of our lips.

Assyria cannot save us; we will not mount war-horses. We will never again say 'Our gods' to what our own hands have made, for in you the fatherless find compassion."

"I will heal their waywardness and love them freely, for my anger has turned away from them." *Hos. 14:1-4*

"Yet you have not called upon me, O Jacob, you have not wearied yourselves for me, O Israel. . . .

"You have not bought any fragrant calamus for me, or lavished on me the fat of your sacrifices. But you have burdened me with your sins and wearied me with your offences.

"I, even I, am he who blots out your transgressions, for my own sake, and remembers your sins no more." *Isa. 43:22, 24-25*

He feeds on ashes, a deluded heart misleads him; he cannot save himself, or say, "Is not this thing in my right hand a lie?"

"Remember these things, O Jacob, for you are my servant, O Israel. I have made you, you are my servant; O Israel, I will not forget you.

"I have swept away your offences like a cloud, your sins like the morning mist. Return to me, for I have redeemed you." *Isa. 44:20-22*

"For I know the plans I have for you," declares the LORD, "plans to prosper you and not to harm you, plans to give you hope and a future. Then you will call upon me and come and pray to me,

and I will listen to you. You will seek me and find
me when you seek me with all your heart."

Jer. 29:11-13

There you will worship man-made gods of
wood and stone, which cannot see or hear or eat
or smell. But if from there you seek the LORD
your God, you will find him if you look for him
with all your heart and with all your soul. When
you are in distress and all these things have happened to you, then in later days you will return to
the LORD your God and obey him. For the LORD
your God is a merciful God; he will not abandon
or destroy you or forget the covenant with your
forefathers, which he confirmed to them by oath.

Deut. 4:28-31

If my people, who are called by my name, will
humble themselves and pray and seek my face
and turn from their wicked ways, then will I hear
from heaven and will forgive their sin and will
heal their land.   *2 Chron. 7:14*

If we confess our sins, he is faithful and just and
will forgive us our sins and purify us from all unrighteousness.   *1 John 1:9*

My dear children, I write this to you so that
you will not sin. But if anybody does sin, we have
one who speaks to the Father in our defence—
Jesus Christ, the Righteous One. He is the atoning sacrifice for our sins, and not only for ours but
also for the sins of the whole world.

1 John 2:1-2

But in their distress they turned to the LORD,
the God of Israel, and sought him, and he was
found by them.   *2 Chron. 15:4*

In his distress he sought the favour of the LORD
his God and humbled himself greatly before the
God of his fathers. And when he prayed to him,
the LORD was moved by his entreaty and listened
to his plea; so he brought him back to Jerusalem

and to his kingdom. Then Manasseh knew that the LORD is God.   *2 Chron. 33:12-13*

Jesus continued: "There was a man who had two sons. The younger one said to his father, 'Father, give me my share of the estate.' So he divided his property between them.

"Not long after that, the younger son got together all he had, set off for a distant country and there squandered his wealth in wild living. After he had spent everything, there was a severe famine in that whole country, and he began to be in need. So he went and hired himself out to a citizen of that country, who sent him to his fields to feed pigs. He longed to fill his stomach with the pods that the pigs were eating, but no-one gave him anything.

"When he came to his senses, he said, 'How many of my father's hired men have food to spare, and here I am starving to death! I will set out and go back to my father and say to him: Father, I have sinned against heaven and against you. I am no longer worthy to be called your son; make me like one of your hired men. So he got up and went to his father.

"But while he was still a long way off, his father saw him and was filled with compassion for him; he ran to his son, threw his arms around him and kissed him.

"The son said to him, 'Father, I have sinned against heaven and against you. I am no longer worthy to be called your son.'

"But the father said to his servants, 'Quick! Bring the best robe and put it on him. Put a ring on his finger and sandals on his feet. Bring the fatted calf and kill it. Let's have a feast and celebrate. For this son of mine was dead and is alive again; he was lost and is found.' So they began to celebrate."   *Luke 15:11-24*

VII. THE BEST TEXTS FOR SKEPTICS

1. Earnest-minded skeptics

"If any one chooses to do God's will, he will find out whether my teaching comes from God or whether I speak on my own."   *John 7:17*

The man without the Spirit does not accept the things that come from the Spirit of God, for they are foolishness to him and he cannot understand them, because they are spiritually discerned.

1 Cor. 2:14

Philip found Nathanael and told him, "We have found the one Moses wrote about in the Law, and about whom the prophets also wrote—Jesus of Nazareth, the son of Joseph."

"Nazareth! Can anything good come from there?" Nathanael asked.

"Come and see," said Philip.

When Jesus saw Nathanael approaching, he said of him, "Here is a true Israelite, in whom there is nothing false."

"How do you know me?" Nathanael asked.

Jesus answered, "I saw you while you were still under the fig-tree before Philip called you."

Then Nathanael declared, "Rabbi, you are the Son of God; you are the King of Israel."

John 1:45-49

Now Thomas (called Didymus), one of the Twelve, was not with the disciples when Jesus came. When the other disciples told him that they had seen the Lord, he declared, "Unless I see the nail marks in his hands and put my finger where the nails were, and put my hand into his side, I will not believe it."

A week later his disciples were in the house again, and Thomas was with them. Though the doors were locked, Jesus came and stood among them, and said, "Peace be with you!" Then he said to Thomas, "Put your finger here; see my hands. Reach out your hand and put it into my side. Stop doubting and believe."

Thomas answered, "My Lord and My God!"

Then Jesus told him, "Because you have seen me, you have believed; blessed are those who have not seen and yet have believed."
John 20:24-29

"No-one ever spoke the way this man does," the guards declared. *John 7:46*

Jesus answered: "Don't you know me, Philip, even after I have been among you such a long time? Anyone who has seen me has seen the Father. How can you say, 'Show us the Father'? Don't you believe that I am in the Father, and that the Father is in me? The words I say to you are not just my own. Rather, it is the Father, living in me, who is doing his work. Believe me when I say that I am in the Father and the Father is in me; or at least believe on the evidence of the miracles themselves." *John 14:9-11*

"He who belongs to God hears what God says. The reason you do not hear is that you do not belong to God." *John 8:47*

"For God did not send his Son into the world to condemn the world, but to save the world through him. Whoever believes in him is not condemned, but whoever does not believe stands condemned already because he has not believed in the name of God's one and only son. This is the verdict: Light has come into the world, but men loved darkness instead of light because their deeds were evil. Everyone who does evil hates the light, and will not come into the light for fear that his deeds will be exposed. But whoever lives by the truth comes into the light, so that it may be seen plainly that what he has done has been done through God." *John 3:17-21*

47

"How can you believe if you accept praise from one another, yet make no effort to obtain the praise that comes from the only God?"

John 5:44

Jesus did many other miraculous signs in the presence of his disciples, which are not recorded in this book. But these are written that you may believe that Jesus is the Christ, the Son of God, and that by believing you may have life in his name. *John 20:30-31*

"If I had not done among them what no-one else did, they would not be guilty of sin. But now they have seen these miracles, and yet they have hated both me and my Father." *John 15:24*

"I too was convinced that I ought to do all that was possible to oppose the name of Jesus of Nazareth. And that is just what I did in Jerusalem. On the authority of the chief priests I put many of the saints in prison, and when they were put to death, I cast my vote against them. Many a time I went from one synagogue to another to have them punished, and I tried to force them to blaspheme. In my obsession against them, I even went to foreign cities to persecute them.

"On one of these journeys I was going to Damascus with the authority and commission of the chief priests. About noon, O king, as I was on the road, I saw a light from heaven, brighter than the sun, blazing around me and my companions. We all fell to the ground, and I heard a voice saying to me in Aramaic, 'Saul, Saul, why do you persecute me? It is hard for you to kick against the goads.'

"Then I asked, 'Who are you, Lord?'

"'I am Jesus, whom you are persecuting,' the Lord replied. 'Now get up and stand on your feet. I have appeared to you to appoint you as a servant and as a witness of what you have seen of me and what I will show you. I will rescue you from your own people and from the Gentiles. I am sending you to open their eyes and turn them from darkness to light, and from the power of Satan to God, so that they may receive forgiveness of sins and a place among those who are sanctified by faith in me.'

"So then, King Agrippa, I was not disobedient to the vision from heaven. First to those in Damascus, then to those in Jerusalem and in all Judea, and to the Gentiles also, I preached that they should repent and turn to God and prove their repentance by their deeds."

Acts 26:9-20

2. Skeptics who are triflers

For the message of the cross is foolishness to those who are perishing, but to us who are being saved it is the power of God.   *1 Cor. 1:18*

And even if our gospel is veiled, it is veiled to those who are perishing. The god of this age has blinded the minds of unbelievers, so that they cannot see the light of the gospel of the glory of Christ, who is the image of God.

2 Cor. 4:3-4

Once more Jesus said to them, "I am going away, and you will look for me, and you will die in your sin. Where I go, you cannot come." . . . "I told you that you would die in your sins; if you do not believe that I am [the one I claim to be], you will indeed die in your sins."   *John 8:21, 24*

. . . And give relief to you who are troubled, and to us as well. This will happen when the Lord Jesus is revealed from heaven in blazing fire with his powerful angels. He will punish those who do not know God and do not obey the gospel of our Lord Jesus.   *2 Thess. 1:7-8*

. . . and in every sort of evil that deceives those who are perishing. They perish because they refused to love the truth and so be saved. For this

49

reason God sends them a powerful delusion so that they will believe the lie and so that all will be condemned who have not believed the truth but have delighted in wickedness.

2 Thess. 2:10-12

Whoever believes and is baptised will be saved, but whoever does not believe will be condemned. *Mark 16:16*

3. Especially for those who doubt the existence of God

. . . Since what may be known about God is plain to them, because God has made it plain to them. For since the creation of the world God's invisible qualities—his eternal power and divine nature—have been clearly seen, being understood from what has been made, so that men are without excuse.

For although they knew God, they neither glorified him as God nor gave thanks to him, but their thinking became futile and their foolish hearts were darkened. Although they claimed to be wise, they became fools. *Rom. 1:19-22*

The heavens declare the glory of God; the skies proclaim the work of his hands. *Ps. 19:1*

The fool says in his heart, "There is no God."

They are corrupt, their deeds are vile; there is no-one who does good. *Ps. 14:1*

4. Those who doubt that the Bible is the Word of God

"Thus you nullify the word of God by your tradition that you have handed down. And you do many things like that." *Mark 7:13*

"Heaven and earth will pass away, but my words will never pass away." *Matt. 24:35*

"I tell you the truth, until heaven and earth disappear, not the smallest letter, not the least

50

stroke of a pen, will by any means disappear from the Law until everything is accomplished."

Matt. 5:18

"If he called them 'gods', to whom the word of God came—and the Scripture cannot be broken—" *John 10:35*

And beginning with Moses and all the Prophets, he explained to them what was said in all the Scriptures concerning himself. . . .
He said to them, "This is what I told you while I was still with you: Everything must be fulfilled that is written about me in the Law of Moses, the Prophets and the Psalms." *Luke 24:27, 44*

And we also thank God continually because, when you received the word of God, which you heard from us, you accepted it not as the word of men, but as it actually is, the word of God, which is at work in you who believe. *1 Thess. 2:13*

And we have the word of the prophets made more certain, and you will do well to pay attention to it, as to a light shining in a dark place, until the day dawns and the morning star rises in your hearts. Above all, you must understand that no prophecy of Scripture came about by the prophet's own interpretation. For prophecy never had its origin in the will of man, but men spoke from God as they were carried along by the Holy Spirit. *2 Peter 1:19-21*

Anyone who believes in the Son of God has this testimony in his heart. Anyone who does not believe God has made him out to be a liar, because he has not believed the testimony God has given about his Son. *1 John 5:10*

"He who belongs to God hears what God says. The reason you do not hear is that you do not belong to God." *John 8:47*

51

5. Those who doubt the divinity of Christ

This is the message God sent to the people of Israel, telling the good news of peace through Jesus Christ, who is Lord of all. *Acts 10:36*

Now instead, you ought to forgive and comfort him, so that he will not be overwhelmed by excessive sorrow. I urge you, therefore, to reaffirm your love for him. *2 Cor. 2:7-8*

But about the Son he says, "Your throne, O God, will last for ever and ever, and righteousness will be the sceptre of your kingdom.

Heb. 1:8

Thomas answered, "My Lord and My God!" Then Jesus told him, "Because you have seen me, you have believed; blessed are those who have not seen and yet have believed."

John 20:28-29

But these are written that you may believe that Jesus is the Christ, the Son of God, and that by believing you may have life in his name.

John 20:31

". . . that all may honour the Son just as they honour the Father. He who does not honour the Son does not honour the Father, who sent him."

John 5:23

Therefore God exalted him to the highest place and gave him the name that is above every name, that at the name of Jesus every knee should bow, in heaven and on earth and under the earth.

Phil. 2:9-10

And again, when God brings his firstborn into the world, he says, "Let all God's angels worship him." *Heb. 1:6*

Who is the liar? It is the man who denies that Jesus is the Christ. Such a man is the antichrist —he denies the Father and the Son. No-one who

denies the Son has the Father; whoever acknowledges the Son has the Father also.

1 John 2:22-23

Everyone who believes that Jesus is the Christ
is born of God, and everyone who loves the father
loves his child as well. This is how we know that
we love the children of God: by loving God and
carrying out his commands. This is love for God:
to obey his commands. And his commands are not
burdensome, for everyone born of God has overcome the world. This is the victory that has overcome the world, even our faith. Who is it that
overcomes the world? Only he who believes that
Jesus is the Son of God. *1 John 5:1-5*

"I told you that you would die in your sins; if
you do not believe that I am [the one I claim to
be], you will indeed die in your sins." *John 8:24*

————

VIII. THE BEST TEXT FOR THOSE WHO WISH TO POSTPONE A DECISION.

Seek the LORD while he may be found; call on
him while he is near.   *Isa. 55:6*

Do not boast about tomorrow, for you do not
know what a day may bring forth.   *Prov. 27:1*

A man who remains stiff-necked after many rebukes will suddenly be destroyed—without rem-
edy.   *Prov. 29:1*

"So you also must be ready, because the Son of
Man will come at an hour when you do not expect
him."   *Matt. 24:44*

"But while they were on their way to buy the
oil, the bridegroom arrived. The virgins who
were ready went in with him to the wedding banquet. And the door was shut.

"Later the others also came. 'Sir! Sir!' they
said, 'Open the door for us!'

"But he replied, 'I tell you the truth, I don't know you.'

"Therefore keep watch, because you do not know the day or the hour."   *Matt. 25:10-13*

"'And I'll say to myself, "You have plenty of good things laid up for many years. Take life easy; eat, drink and be merry."'

"But God said to him, 'You fool! This very night your life will be demanded from you. Then who will get what you have prepared for yourself?'"
Luke 12:19-20

Elijah went before the people and said, "How long will you waver between two opinions? If the LORD is God, follow him; but if Baal is God, follow him."   *1 Kings 18:21*

Now listen, you who say, "Today or tomorrow we will go to this or that city, spend a year there, carry on business and make money." Why, you do not even know what will happen tomorrow. What is your life? You are a mist that appears for a little while and then vanishes.   *James 4:13-14*

"Make every effort to enter through the narrow door, because many, I tell you, will try to enter and will not be able to. Once the owner of the house gets up and closes the door, you will stand outside knocking and pleading, 'Sir, open the door for us.'

"But he will answer, 'I don't know you or where you come from.'"   *Luke 13:24-25*

Then Jesus told them, "You are going to have the light just a little while longer. Walk while you have the light, before darkness overtakes you. The man who walks in the dark does not know where he is going."   *John 12:35*

"But seek first his kingdom and his righteousness, and all these things will be given to you as well, Therefore do not worry about tomorrow, for tomorrow will worry about itself. Each day has enough trouble of its own."   *Matt. 6:33-34*

"At the time of my favour I heard you, and on the day of salvation I helped you."

I tell you, now is the time of God's favour, now is the day of salvation.   *2 Cor. 6:2*

As has just been said: "Today, if you hear his voice, do not harden your hearts as you did in the rebellion."   *Heb. 3:15*

Remember your Creator in the days of your youth, before the days of trouble come and the years approach when you will say, "I find no pleasure in them"—   *Eccl. 12:1*

———

IX. THE BEST TEXTS FOR ROMAN CATHOLICS.

In reply Jesus declared, "I tell you the truth, unless a man is born again, he cannot see the kingdom of God."

Jesus answered, "I tell you the truth, unless a man is born of water and the Spirit, he cannot enter the kingdom of God. . . . You should not be surprised at my saying, 'You must be born again.'"   *John 3:3, 5, 7*

If you know that he is righteous, you know that everyone who does what is right has been born of him.   *1 John 2:29*

No-one who is born of God will continue to sin, because God's seed remains in him; he cannot go on sinning, because he has been born of God. . . .

We know that we have passed from death to life, because we love our brothers. Anyone who does not love remains in death. Anyone who hates his brother is a murderer, and you know that no murderer has eternal life in him.

This is how we know what love is: Jesus Christ laid down his life for us. And we ought to lay down our lives for our brothers. If anyone has material possessions and sees his brother in need but has no pity on him, how can the love of God be in him?   *1 John 3:9, 14-17*

For everyone born of God has overcome the world. This is the victory that has overcome the world, even our faith.   *1 John 5:4*

They replied, "Believe in the Lord Jesus, and you will be saved—you and your household."
                                        Acts 16:31

However, to the man who does not work but trusts God who justifies the wicked, his faith is credited as righteousness.   *Rom. 4:5*

For there is one God and one mediator between God and men, the man Christ Jesus.
                                        1 Tim. 2:5

Then I acknowledged my sin to you and did not cover up my iniquity. I said, "I will confess . . ."
                                        Ps. 32:5

I write these things to you who believe in the name of the Son of God so that you may know that you have eternal life.   *1 John 5:13*

Through him everyone who believes is justified from everything you could not be justified from by the law of Moses.   *Acts 13:39*

"You diligently study the Scriptures because you think that by them you possess eternal life. These are the Scriptures that testify about me."
                                        John 5:39

Therefore, rid yourselves of all malice and all deceit, hypocrisy, envy, and slander of every kind. Like newborn babies, crave pure spiritual milk, so that by it you may grow up in your salvation.   *1 Peter 2:1, 2*

. . . while evil men and impostors will go from bad to worse, deceiving and being deceived. But as for you, continue in what you have learned and have become convinced of, because you know those from whom you learned it, and how from infancy you have known the holy Scriptures, which are able to make you wise for salvation through faith in Christ Jesus. All Scripture is God-breathed and is useful for teaching, rebuking, correcting and training in righteousness, so that the man of God may be thoroughly equipped for every good work. *2 Tim. 3:13-17*

" 'They worship me in vain; their teachings are but rules taught by men.' You have let go of the commands of God and are holding on to the traditions of men. . . . Thus you nullify the word of God by your tradition that you have handed down. And you do many things like that."
Mark 7:7-8, 13

Jesus replied, "You are in error because you do not know the Scriptures or the power of God."
Matt. 22:29

X. THE BEST TEXT FOR JEWS

Who has believed our message and to whom has the arm of the LORD been revealed?

He grew up before him like a tender shoot, and like a root out of dry ground.

He had no beauty or majesty to attract us to him, nothing in his appearance that we should desire him.

He was despised and rejected by men, a man of sorrows, and familiar with suffering.

Like one from whom men hide their faces he was despised, and we esteemed him not.

Surely he took up our infirmities and carried our sorrows, yet we considered him stricken by God, smitten by him, and afflicted.

But he was pierced for our transgressions, he was crushed for our iniquities; the punishment that brought us peace was upon him, and by his wounds we are healed.

We all, like sheep, have gone astray, each of us has turned to his own way; and the Lord has laid on him the iniquity of us all.

He was oppressed and afflicted, yet he did not open his mouth; he was led like a lamb to the slaughter, and as a sheep before her shearers is silent, so he did not open his mouth.

By oppression and judgment, he was taken away. And who can speak of his descendants?

For he was cut off from the land of the living; for the transgression of my people he was stricken.

He was assigned a grave with the wicked, and with the rich in his death, though he had done no violence, nor was any deceit in his mouth.

Yet it was the LORD's will to crush him and cause him to suffer, and though the LORD makes his life a guilt offering, he will see his offspring and prolong his days, and the will of the LORD will prosper in his hand.

After the suffering of his soul, he will see the light [of life] and be satisfied; by his knowledge my righteous servant will justify many, and he will bear their iniquities.

Therefore I will give him a portion among the great, and he will divide the spoils with the strong, because he poured out his life unto death, and was numbered with the transgressors.

For he bore the sin of many, and made intercession for the transgressors.   *Isa. 53*

"And I will pour out on the house of David and the inhabitants of Jerusalem a spirit of grace and supplication. They will look on me, the one they have pierced, and mourn for him as one mourns for an only child, and grieve bitterly for him as one grieves for a firstborn son."   *Zech. 12:10*

"After the sixty-two 'sevens,' the Anointed One will be cut off and will have nothing. The people of the ruler who will come will destroy the city and the sanctuary. The end will come like a flood: War will continue until the end, and desolations have been decreed."

Dan. 9:26

XI. THE BEST TEXTS FOR SPIRITUALISTS

When men tell you to consult mediums and spiritists, who whisper and mutter, should not a people enquire of their God? Why consult the dead on behalf of the living? To the law and to the testimony! If they do not speak according to this word, they have no light of dawn.

Isa. 8:19-20

Dear friends, do not believe every spirit, but test the spirits to see whether they are from God, because many false prophets have gone out into the world. . . . but every spirit that does not acknowledge Jesus is not from God. This is the spirit of the antichrist, which you have heard is coming and even now is already in the world.

1 John 4:1, 3

"'Do not turn to mediums or seek out spiritists, for you will be defiled by them. I am the LORD your God."

Lev. 19:31

"I will set my face against the person who turns to mediums and spiritists to prostitute himself by following them, and I will cut him off from his people."

Lev. 20:6

Let no-one be found among you who sacrifices his son or daughter in the fire, who practises divination or sorcery, interprets omens, engages in witchcraft, or casts spells, or who is a medium or spiritist or who consults the dead. Anyone who does these things is detestable to the LORD, and because of these detestable practices the LORD your God will drive out those nations before you.

Deut. 18:10-12

The coming of the lawless one will be in accordance with the work of Satan displayed in all kinds of counterfeit miracles, signs and wonders, and in every sort of evil that deceives those who are perishing. They perish because they refused to love the truth and so be saved. For this reason God sends them a powerful delusion so that they will believe the lie and so that all will be condemned who have not believed the truth but have delighted in wickedness.

2 Thess. 2:9-12

Manasseh was twelve years old when he became king, and he reigned in Jerusalem for fifty-five years. His mother's name was Hephzibah. He did evil in the eyes of the LORD, following the detestable practices of the nations the LORD had driven out before the Israelites. . . .

He sacrificed his own son in the fire, practised sorcery and divination, and consulted mediums and spiritists. He did much evil in the eyes of the LORD, provoking him to anger.

2 Kings 21:1, 2, 6

Saul died because he was unfaithful to the LORD; he did not keep the word of the LORD, and even consulted a medium for guidance and did not enquire of the LORD. So the LORD put him to death and turned the kingdom over to David son of Jesse.   *1 Chron. 10:13-14*

XII. THE BEST TEXTS FOR JEHOVAH'S WITNESSES

1. The Bible as God's Revelation

Above all, you must understand that no prophecy of Scripture came about by the prophet's own interpretation. For prophecy never had its origin in the will of man, but men spoke from God as they were carried along by the Holy Spirit.

2 Peter 1:20-21

But as for you, continue in what you have learned and have become convinced of, because you know those from whom you learned it, and how from infancy you have known the holy Scriptures, which are able to make you wise for salvation through faith in Christ Jesus. All Scripture is God-breathed and is useful for teaching, rebuking, correcting and training in righteousness, so that the man of God may be thoroughly equipped for every good work.

2 Tim. 3:14-17

I warn everyone who hears the words of the prophecy of this book: If anyone adds anything to them, God will add to him the plagues described in this book. And if anyone takes words away from this book of prophecy, God will take away from him his share in the tree of life and in the holy city, which are described in this book.

Rev. 22:18-19

2. The deity of Christ

God said to Moses, "I am who I am. This is what you are to say to the Israelites: 'I AM has sent me to you.'"

Exod. 3:14

"I tell you the truth," Jesus answered, "before Abraham was born, I am!"

John 8:58

In the beginning was the Word, and the Word was with God, and the Word was God. He was with God in the beginning. . . . The Word became flesh and lived for a while among us. We have seen his glory, the glory of the one and only [Son], who came from the Father, full of grace and truth.

John 1:1-2, 14

"All things have been committed to me by my Father. No one knows the Son except the Father, and no one knows the Father except the Son and those to whom the Son chooses to reveal him."

Matt. 11:27

Dear friends, do not believe every spirit, but test the spirits to see whether they are from God, because many false prophets have gone out into the world. This is how you can recognise the Spirit of God: Every spirit that acknowledges that Jesus Christ has come in the flesh is from God, but every spirit that does not acknowledge Jesus is not from God.

1 John 4:1-3

3. Man accountable for sins

It is written: "'As surely as I live,' says the Lord, 'Every knee will bow before me; every tongue will confess to God.'" So then, each of us will give an account of himself to God.

Rom. 14:11-12

"The soul who sins is the one who will die. The son will not share the guilt of the father, nor will the father share the guilt of the son. The righteousness of the righteous man will be credited to him, and the wickedness of the wicked will be charged against him."

Ezek. 18:20

For the wages of sin is death, but the gift of God is eternal life in Christ Jesus our Lord.

Rom. 6:23

4. Atonement and eternal life through Christ

For what I received I passed on to you as of first importance: that Christ died for our sins according to the Scriptures, that he was buried, that he was raised on the third day according to the Scriptures.

1 Cor. 15:3-4

But he was pierced for our transgressions, he was crushed for our iniquities; the punishment that brought us peace was upon him, and by his wounds we are healed. We all, like sheep, have gone astray, each of us has turned to his own way;

and the LORD has laid on him the iniquity of us all. . . . Yet it was the LORD's will to crush him and cause him to suffer, and though the LORD makes his life a guilt offering, he will see his off-spring and prolong his days, and the will of the LORD will prosper in his hand. *Isa. 53:5-6, 10*

"On that day a fountain will be opened to the house of David and the inhabitants of Jerusalem, to cleanse them from sin and impurity."
Zech. 13:1

But if we walk in the light, as he is in the light, we have fellowship with one another, and the blood of Jesus, his Son, purifies us from every sin. If we claim to be without sin, we deceive ourselves and the truth is not in us. If we confess our sins, he is faithful and just and will forgive us our sins and purify us from all unrighteousness.
1 John 1:7-9

Here is a trustworthy saying that deserves full acceptance: Christ Jesus came into the world to save sinners—of whom I am the worst. But for that very reason I was shown mercy so that in me, the worst of sinners, Christ Jesus might display his unlimited patience as an example for those who would believe on him and receive eternal life. *1 Tim. 1:15-16*

At just the right time, when we were still pow-erless, Christ died for the ungodly. . . . But God demonstrates his own love for us in this: While we were still sinners, Christ died for us.
Rom. 5:6, 8

"My sheep listen to my voice; I know them, and they follow me. I give them eternal life, and they shall never perish; no-one can snatch them out of my hand. My Father, who has given them to me, is greater than all; no-one can snatch them out of my Father's hand. I and the Father are one." *John 10:27-30*

5. Salvation by faith and not works

For it is by grace you have been saved, through faith—and this not from yourselves, it is the gift of God—not by works, so that no-one can boast.
Eph. 2:8-9

Then they asked him, "What must we do to do the works God requires?" Jesus answered, "The work of God is this: to believe in the one he has sent."
John 6:28-29

In the gospel a righteousness from God is revealed, a righteousness that is by faith from first to last, just as it is written: "The righteous will live by faith."
Rom. 1:17

If, in fact, Abraham was justified by works, he had something to boast about—but not before God. What does the Scripture say? "Abraham believed God, and it was credited to him as righteousness."
Rom. 4:2-3

6. The certainty of the future state of man

"Do not be amazed at this, for a time is coming when all who are in their graves will hear his voice and come out—those who have done good will rise to live, and those who have done evil will rise to be condemned."
John 5:28-29

"But Abraham replied, 'Son, remember that in your lifetime you received your good things, while Lazarus received bad things, but now he is comforted here and you are in agony. And besides all this, between us and you a great chasm has been fixed, so that those who want to go from here to you cannot, nor can anyone cross over from there to us.'"
Luke 16:25-26

This will happen when the Lord Jesus is revealed from heaven in blazing fire with his powerful angels. He will punish those who do not know God and do not obey the gospel of our Lord Jesus. They will be punished with everlasting destruction and shut out from the presence of the Lord and from the majesty of his power on the day he comes to be glorified in his holy people and to be marvelled at among all those who have believed. *2 Thess. 1:7-10*

"If your hand causes you to sin, cut it off. It is better for you to enter life maimed than with two hands to go into hell, where the fire never goes out." *Mark 9:43*

The lake of fire is the second death. If anyone's name was not found written in the book of life, he was thrown into the lake of fire. *Rev. 20:14-15*

He said to me: "It is done. I am the Alpha and the Omega, the Beginning and the End. To him who is thirsty I will give to drink without cost from the spring of the water of life. He who overcomes will inherit all this, and I will be his God and he will be my son. But the cowardly, the unbelieving, the vile, the murderers, the sexually immoral, those who practise magic arts, the idolaters and all liars—their place will be in the fiery lake of burning sulphur. This is the second death." *Rev. 21:6-8*

XIII. THE BEST TEXTS FOR MORMONS

1. One God, transcendent to man

"I am the LORD; that is my name! I will not give my glory to another or my praise to idols." *Isa. 42:8*

"This is what the LORD says—Israel's King and Redeemer, the LORD Almighty: I am the first and I am the last; apart from me there is no God. Who then is like me? . . . You are my witnesses. Is there any God besides me? No, there is no other Rock; I know not one."   *Isa. 44:6-8*

"For I am God, and not man—the Holy One among you."   *Hos. 11:9*

2. Christ the only Saviour

"It is by the name of Jesus Christ of Nazareth, whom you crucified but whom God raised from the dead, that this man stands before you completely healed. . . . Salvation is found in no-one else, for there is no other name under heaven given to men by which we must be saved."
Acts 4:10-12

"Whoever believes in the Son has eternal life, but whoever rejects the Son will not see life, for God's wrath remains on him."   *John 3:36*

Grace and peace to you from God our Father and the Lord Jesus Christ, who gave himself for our sins to rescue us from the present evil age, according to the will of our God and Father.
Gal. 1:3-4

3. The sinfulness of man

There is not a righteous man on earth who does what is right and never sins.   *Eccl. 7:20*

This righteousness from God comes through faith in Jesus Christ to all who believe. There is no difference, for all have sinned and fall short of the glory of God, and are justified freely by his grace through the redemption that came by Christ Jesus.   *Rom. 3:22-24*

Therefore, just as sin entered the world through one man, and death through sin, and in this way death came to all men, because all sinned.   *Rom. 5:12*

"There is no-one righteous, not even one; there is no-one who understands, no-one who seeks God."   *Rom. 3:11-12*

4. Salvation by faith, not works

In the gospel a righteousness from God is revealed, a righteousness that is by faith from first to last, just as it is written: "The righteous will live by faith." *Rom. 1:17*

All who rely on observing the law are under a curse, for it is written: "Cursed is everyone who does not continue to do everything written in the Book of the Law." Clearly no-one is justified before God by the law, because, "The righteous will live by faith." *Gal. 3:10-11*

But when the kindness and love of God our Saviour appeared, he saved us, not because of righteous things we had done, but because of his mercy. *Titus 3:4-5*

For it is by grace you have been saved, through faith—and this not from yourselves, it is the gift of God—not by works, so that no-one can boast. *Eph. 2:8-9*

Then they asked him, "What must we do to do the works God requires?" Jesus answered, "The work of God is this: to believe in the one he has sent." *John 6:28-29*

5. Priesthood of believers and high priesthood of Christ

As you come to him, the living Stone—rejected by men but chosen by God and precious to him—you also, like living stones, are being built into a spiritual house to be a holy priesthood, offering spiritual sacrifices acceptable to God through Jesus Christ. *1 Peter 2:4-5*

For it is declared: "You are a priest for ever, in the order of Melchizedek." The former regulation is set aside because it was weak and useless (for the law made nothing perfect), and a better hope is introduced, by which we draw near to God.
And it was not without an oath! Others became

priests without any oath, but he became a priest with an oath when God said to him: "The Lord has sworn and will not change his mind: 'You are a priest for ever.'" Because of this oath, Jesus has become the guarantee of a better covenant. . . .

Therefore he is able to save completely those who come to God through him, because he always lives to intercede for them.

Heb. 7:17-22, 25

This is good, and pleases God our Saviour, who wants all men to be saved and to come to a knowledge of the truth. For there is one God and one mediator between God and men, the man Christ Jesus, who gave himself as a ransom for all men—the testimony given in its proper time.

1 Tim. 2:3-6

XIV. BEST SCRIPTURES FOR THOSE INVOLVED WITH CULTS

Use also passages in I, II, and IX.

1. Essential issues common to cults

a. *No leader given unique authority from God*

Above all, you must understand that no prophecy of Scripture came about by the prophet's own interpretation. For prophecy never had its origin in the will of man, but men spoke from God as they were carried along by the Holy Spirit.

2 Peter 1:20-21

b. *Salvation not through works*

For it is by grace you have been saved, through faith—and this not from yourselves, it is the gift of God—not by works, so that no-one can boast.

Eph. 2:8-9

c. *Salvation only through belief in Jesus Christ*

And this is the testimony: God has given us

eternal life, and this life is in his Son. He who has the Son has life; he who does not have the Son of God does not have life. *1 John 5:11-12*

But these are written that you may believe that Jesus is the Christ, the Son of God, and that by believing you may have life in his name.

John 20:31

2. For those involved in cults based on Western religions

a. The Holy Spirit truly God

But God has revealed it to us by his Spirit. The Spirit searches all things, even the deep things of God. For who among men knows the thoughts of a man except the man's spirit within him? In the same way no-one knows the thoughts of God except the Spirit of God. We have not received the spirit of the world but the Spirit who is from God, that we may understand what God has freely given us. *1 Cor. 2:10-12*

b. Jesus Christ truly God

In the past God spoke to our forefathers through the prophets at many times and in various ways, but in these last days he has spoken to us by his Son, whom he appointed heir of all things, and through whom he made the universe.

Heb. 1:1-2

c. Jesus Christ successful in His mission on earth

For Christ did not enter a man-made sanctuary that was only a copy of the true one; he entered heaven itself, now to appear for us in God's presence. Nor did he enter heaven to offer himself again and again, the way the high priest enters the Most Holy Place every year with blood that is not his own. Then Christ would have had to suffer many times since the creation of the world. But now he has appeared once for all at the end of the ages to do away with sin by the sacrifice of himself. Just as man is destined to die once, and after that to face judgment, so Christ was sacrificed once to take away the sins of many people; and he will appear a second time, not to bear sin, but to bring salvation to those who are waiting for him.

Heb. 9:24-28

3. For those involved in Eastern religions and cults

a. As to beliefs held in common in Eastern religions

—*God distinct from creation and not a part of everything*

In the beginning God created the heavens and the earth. *Gen. 1:1*

—*God and Christ not created, but always existent*

In the beginning was the Word, and the Word was with God, and the Word was God. He was with God in the beginning. Through him all things were made; without him nothing was made that has been made. *John 1:1-3*

—*God not a part of a human being until there is faith in Christ*

This righteousness from God comes through faith in Jesus Christ to all who believe. There is no difference, for all have sinned and fall short of the glory of God. *Rom. 3:22-23*

b. For those involved in Transcendental Meditation

—*Ignorance of God, not self, the problem of humanity*

What shall we conclude then? Are we any better? Not at all! We have already made the charge that Jews and Gentiles alike are all under sin. As it is written: "There is no-one righteous, not even one; there is no-one who understands, no-one who seeks God. All have turned away, they have together become worthless; there is no-one who does good, not even one." *Rom. 3:9-12*

—Happiness arising from serving God, not from mindlessness

"Blessed are those who hunger and thirst for righteousness, for they will be filled."

Matt. 5:6

"But seek first his kingdom and his righteousness, and all these things will be given to you as well."

Matt. 6:33

c. For those involved with Krishna Consciousness

—People born as human beings with only one life on earth; not reincarnated

Man is destined to die once, and after that to face judgment. *Heb. 9:27*

"Do not be amazed at this, for a time is coming when all who are in their graves will hear his voice and come out—those who have done good will rise to live, and those who have done evil will rise to be condemned." *John 5:28-29*

—Jesus a blameless and perfect Saviour

Such a high priest meets our need—one who is holy, blameless, pure, set apart from sinners, exalted above the heavens. Unlike the other high priests, he does not need to offer sacrifices day after day, first for his own sins, and then for the sins of the people. He sacrificed for their sins once for all when he offered himself.

Heb. 7:26-27

For we do not have a high priest who is unable to sympathise with our weaknesses, but we have one who has been tempted in every way, just as we are—yet was without sin.   *Heb. 4:15*

XV. THE BEST TEXTS FOR CHRISTIANS WHO NEED HELP

1. For Christians who are neglecting the open confession of Christ

"Whoever acknowledges me before men, I will also acknowledge him before my Father in heaven. But whoever disowns me before men, I will disown him before my Father in heaven."
                                        Matt. 10:32-33

That if you confess with your mouth, "Jesus is Lord," and believe in your heart that God raised him from the dead, you will be saved.

For it is with your heart that you believe and are justified, and it is with your mouth that you confess and are saved.   *Rom. 10:9-10*

Yet at the same time many even among the leaders believed in him. But because of the Pharisees they would not confess their faith for fear they would be put out of the synagogue; for they loved praise from men more than praise from God.   *John 12:42-43*

"If anyone is ashamed of me and my words in this adulterous and sinful generation, the Son of Man will be ashamed of him when he comes in his Father's glory with the holy angels." *Mark 8:38*

2. For Christians who are neglecting the Bible

Like newborn babies, crave pure spiritual milk, so that by it you may grow up in your salvation.   *1 Peter 2:2*

"Now I commit you to God and to the word of his grace, which can build you up and give you an inheritance among all those who are sanctified."
                                        Acts 20:32

Therefore, get rid of all moral filth and the evil that is so prevalent, and humbly accept the word planted in you, which can save you.

Do not merely listen to the word, and so deceive yourselves. Do what it says. *James 1:21-22*

. . . while evil men and impostors will go from bad to worse, deceiving and being deceived. But as for you, continue in what you have learned and have become convinced of, because you know those from whom you learned it, and how from infancy you have known the holy Scriptures, which are able to make you wise for salvation through faith in Christ Jesus. All Scripture is God-breathed and is useful for teaching, rebuking, correcting and training in righteousness, so that the man of God may be thoroughly equipped for every good work. *2 Tim. 3:13-17*

Take the helmet of salvation and the sword of the Spirit, which is the word of God.

Eph. 6:17

How can a young man keep his way pure? By living according to your word. . . .

I have hidden your word in my heart that I might not sin against you. . . .

The entrance of your words gives light; it gives understanding to the simple. *Ps. 119:9, 11, 130*

Blessed is the man who does not walk in the counsel of the wicked or stand in the way of sinners or sit in the seat of mockers.

But his delight is in the law of the LORD, and on his law he meditates day and night. *Ps. 1:1-2*

Do not let this Book of the Law depart from your mouth; meditate on it day and night, so that you may be careful to do everything written in it. Then you will be prosperous and successful.

Josh. 1:8

Now the Bereans were of more noble character than the Thessalonians, for they received the message with great eagerness and examined the Scriptures every day to see if what Paul said was true. *Acts 17:11*

3. For Christians who are neglecting prayer

You want something but don't get it. You kill and covet, but you cannot have what you want. You quarrel and fight. You do not have, because you do not ask God. *James 4:2*

"So I say to you: Ask and it will be given to you; seek and you will find; knock and the door will be opened to you. For everyone who asks receives; he who seeks finds; and to him who knocks, the door will be opened.

"Which of you fathers, if your son asks for a fish, will give him a snake instead? Or if he asks for an egg, will give him a scorpion? If you then, though you are evil, know how to give good gifts to your children, how much more will your Father in heaven give the Holy Spirit to those who ask him!" *Luke 11:9-13*

Is any one of you in trouble? He should pray. Is anyone happy? Let him sing songs of praise. Is any one of you sick? He should call the elders of the church to pray over him and anoint him with oil in the name of the Lord. And the prayer offered in faith will make the sick person well; the Lord will raise him up. If he has sinned, he will be forgiven. Therefore confess your sins to each other and pray for each other so that you may be healed. The prayer of a righteous man is powerful and effective. Elijah was a man just like us. He prayed earnestly that it would not rain, and it did not rain on the land for three and a half years. Again he prayed, and the heavens gave rain, and the earth produced its crops. *James 5:13-18*

"Why are you sleeping?" he asked them. "Get up and pray so that you will not fall into temptation." *Luke 22:46*

74

But those who hope in the LORD will renew their strength.

They will soar on wings like eagles; they will run and not grow weary, they will walk and not be faint. *Isa. 40:31*

Evening, morning and noon I cry out in distress, and he hears my voice. *Ps. 55:17*

Now when Daniel learned that the decree had been published, he went home to his upstairs room where the windows opened towards Jerusalem. Three times a day he got down on his knees and prayed, giving thanks to his God, just as he had done before. *Dan. 6:10*

One of those days Jesus went out into the hills to pray, and spent the night praying to God. *Luke 6:12*

Pray continually. *1 Thess. 5:17*

4. For Christians who are living careless lives

Do not be yoked together with unbelievers. For what do righteousness and wickedness have in common? Or what fellowship can light have with darkness? What harmony is there between Christ and Belial? What does a believer have in common with an unbeliever? What agreement is there between the temple of God and idols? For we are the temple of the living God. As God has said: "I will live with them and walk among them, and I will be their God, and they will be my people."

"Therefore come out from them and be separate, says the Lord. Touch no unclean thing, and I will receive you."

"I will be a Father to you, and you will be my sons and daughters, says the Lord Almighty."

Since we have these promises, dear friends, let us purify ourselves from everything that contaminates body and spirit, perfecting holiness out of reverence for God. *2 Cor. 6:14–7:1*

"No-one can serve two masters. Either he will hate the one and love the other, or he will be devoted to the one and despise the other. You cannot serve both God and Money.

Matt. 6:24

Do not love the world or anything in the world. If anyone loves the world, the love of the Father is not in him. For everything in the world—the cravings of sinful man, the lust of his eyes and the boasting of what he has and does—comes not from the Father but from the world. The world and its desires pass away, but the man who does the will of God lives for ever. *1 John 2:15-17*

You adulterous people, don't you know that friendship with the world is hatred towards God? Anyone who chooses to be a friend of the world becomes an enemy of God. . . . but he gives us more grace? That is why Scripture says:

"God opposes the proud but gives grace to the humble."

Submit yourselves, then, to God. Resist the devil, and he will flee from you. Come near to God and he will come near to you. Wash your hands, you sinners, and purify your hearts, you who are double-minded. *James 4:4, 6-8*

Make every effort to live in peace with all men and to be holy; without holiness no-one will see the Lord. *Heb. 12:14*

Therefore, prepare your minds for action; be self-controlled; set your hope fully on the grace to be given you when Jesus Christ is revealed. As obedient children, do not conform to the evil desires you had when you lived in ignorance. But just as he who called you is holy, so be holy in all you do; for it is written: "Be holy, because I am holy."

Since you call on a Father who judges each man's work impartially, live your lives as strangers here in reverent fear. For you know that it was not with perishable things such as silver or gold that you were redeemed from the empty way of life handed down to you from your forefathers, but with the precious blood of Christ, a lamb without blemish or defect.   *1 Peter 1:13-19*

For it is time for judgment to begin with the family of God; and if it begins with us, what will the outcome be for those who do not obey the gospel of God? And, "If it is hard for the righteous to be saved, what will become of the ungodly and the sinner?"   *1 Peter 4:17-18*

"The seed that fell among thorns stands for those who hear, but as they go on their way they are choked by life's worries, riches and pleasures, and they do not mature."   *Luke 8:14*

"Be careful, or your hearts will be weighed down with dissipation, drunkenness and the anxieties of life, and that day will close on you unexpectedly like a trap. For it will come upon all those who live on the face of the whole earth. Be always on the watch, and pray that you may be able to escape all that is about to happen, and that you may be able to stand before the Son of Man."
          Luke 21:34-36

"Be dressed ready for service and keep your lamps burning, like men waiting for their master to return from a wedding banquet, so that when he comes and knocks they can immediately open the door for him. It will be good for those servants whose master finds them watching when he comes. I tell you the truth, he will dress himself to serve, will have them recline at the table and will come and wait on them. It will be good for those servants whose master finds them ready, even if he comes in the second or third watch of the night."   *Luke 12:35-38*

Therefore, I urge you, brothers, in view of God's mercy, to offer your bodies as living sacrifices, holy and pleasing to God—which is your spiritual worship. Do not conform any longer to the pattern of this world, but be transformed by the renewing of your mind. Then you will be able to test and approve what God's will is—his good, pleasing and perfect will.

Rom. 12:1-2

But the man who has doubts is condemned if he eats, because his eating is not from faith; and everything that does not come from faith is sin.

Rom. 14:23

I have fought the good fight, I have finished the race, I have kept the faith. Now there is in store for me the crown of righteousness, which the Lord, the righteous Judge, will award to me on that day—and not only to me, but also to all who have longed for his appearing.   *2 Tim. 4:7-8*

5. For Christians who are not working for Christ

"It's like a man going away: He leaves his house in charge of his servants, each with his assigned task, and tells the one at the door to keep watch.

"Therefore keep watch because you do not know when the owner of the house will come back—whether in the evening, or at midnight, or when the cock crows, or at dawn. If he comes suddenly, do not let him find you sleeping. What I say to you, I say to everyone: 'Watch!'"

Mark 13:34-37

"So you also must be ready, because the Son of Man will come at an hour when you do not expect him.

"Who then is the faithful and wise servant, whom the master has put in charge of the servants in his household to give them their food at the proper time? It will be good for that servant whose master finds him doing so when he returns. I tell you the truth, he will put him in charge of all his possessions. But suppose that servant is wicked and says to himself, 'My master is staying away a long time,' and he then begins to beat his fellow servants and to eat and drink with drunkards. The master of that servant will come on a day when he does not expect him and at an hour he is not aware of. He will cut him to pieces and assign him a place with the hypocrites, where there will be weeping and gnashing of teeth."

Matt. 24:44-51

"Again, it will be like a man going on a journey, who called his servants and entrusted his property to them. To one he gave five talents of money, to another two talents, and to another one talent, each according to his ability. Then he went on his journey. The man who had received the five talents went at once and put his money to work and gained five more. So also, the one with the two talents gained two more. But the man who had received the one talent went off, dug a hole in the ground and hid his master's money.

"After a long time the master of those servants returned and settled accounts with them. The man who had received the five talents brought the other five. 'Master,' he said, 'you entrusted me with five talents. See, I have gained five more.'

"His master replied, 'Well done, good and faithful servant! You have been faithful with a few things; I will put you in charge of many things. Come and share your master's happiness!'

"The man with the two talents also came. 'Master,' he said, 'you entrusted me with two talents; see, I have gained two more.'

"His master replied, 'Well done, good and faithful servant! You have been faithful with a few things; I will put you in charge of many things. Come and share your master's happiness!'

"Then the man who had received the one talent came. 'Master,' he said, 'I knew that you are a hard man, harvesting where you have not sown and gathering where you have not scattered seed. So I was afraid and went out and hid your talent in the ground. See, here is what belongs to you.'

"His master replied, 'You wicked, lazy servant! So you knew that I harvest where I have not sown and gather where I have not scattered seed? Well then, you should have put my money on deposit with the bankers, so that when I returned I would have received it back with interest.

" 'Take the talent from him and give it to the one who has the ten talents. For everyone who has will be given more, and he will have an abundance. Whoever does not have, even what he has will be taken from him. And throw that worthless servant outside, into the darkness, where there will be weeping and gnashing of teeth.' "

Matt. 25:14-30

Those who had been scattered preached the word wherever they went. *Acts 8:4*

Then we will no longer be infants, tossed back and forth by the waves, and blown here and there by every wind of teaching and by the cunning and craftiness of men in their deceitful scheming. Instead, speaking the truth in love, we will in all things grow up into him who is the Head, that is, Christ. From him the whole body, joined and held together by every supporting ligament, grows and builds itself up in love, as each part does its work. *Eph. 4:14-16*

. . . for it is light that makes everything visible. This is why it is said:
"Wake up, O sleeper, rise from the dead, and Christ will shine on you."
Be very careful, then, how you live—not as unwise but as wise, making the most of every opportunity, because the days are evil. Therefore do not be foolish, but understand what the Lord's will is. Do not get drunk on wine, which leads to debauchery. Instead, be filled with the Spirit.

Speak to one another with psalms, hymns and spiritual songs. Sing and make music in your heart to the Lord, always giving thanks to God the Father for everything, in the name of our Lord Jesus Christ.

Submit to one another out of reverence for Christ. *Eph. 5:14-21*

"She did what she could." *Mark 14:8*

. . . remember this: Whoever turns a sinner away from his error will save him from death and cover over a multitude of sins. *James 5:20*

Those who are wise will shine like the brightness of the heavens, and those who lead many to righteousness, like the stars for ever and ever.
Dan. 12:3

"Behold, I am coming soon! My reward is with me, and I will give to everyone according to what he has done. I am the Alpha and the Omega, the First and the Last, the Beginning and the End."
Rev. 22:12

6. For Christians who are undergoing temptation

Consider it pure joy, my brothers, whenever you face trials of many kinds, because you know that the testing of your faith develops perseverance. Perseverance must finish its work so that you may be mature and complete, not lacking anything. *James 1:2-4*

Blessed is the man who perseveres under trial, because when he has stood the test, he will receive the crown of life that God has promised to those who love him. *James 1:12*

Be self-controlled and alert. Your enemy the devil prowls around like a roaring lion looking for someone to devour. Resist him, standing firm in the faith, because you know that your brothers throughout the world are undergoing the same kind of sufferings.

And the God of all grace, who called you to his eternal glory in Christ, after you have suffered a little while, will himself restore you and make you strong, firm and steadfast. To him be the power for ever and ever. Amen.   *1 Peter 5:8-11*

No temptation has seized you except what is common to man. And God is faithful; he will not let you be tempted beyond what you can bear. But when you are tempted, he will also provide a way out so that you can stand up under it.
1 Cor. 10:13

But he said to me, "My grace is sufficient for you, for my power is made perfect in weakness." Therefore I will boast all the more gladly about my weaknesses, so that Christ's power may rest on me. That is why, for Christ's sake, I delight in weaknesses, in insults, in hardships, in persecutions, in difficulties. For when I am weak, then I am strong.   *2 Cor. 12:9-10*

Pray continually.   *1 Thess. 5:17*

He gives strength to the weary and increases the power of the weak.

Even youths grow tired and weary, and young men stumble and fall; but those who hope in the LORD will renew their strength.

They will soar on wings like eagles; they will run and not grow weary, they will walk and not be faint.   *Isa. 40:29-31*

I can do everything through him who gives me strength.   *Phil. 4:13*

I write to you, fathers, because you have known him who is from the beginning.

I write to you, young men, because you are strong, and the word of God lives in you, and you have overcome the evil one.   *1 John 2:14*

How can a young man keep his way pure? By living according to your word.   *Ps. 119:9*

7. For Christians who are undergoing persecution

"Blessed are those who are persecuted because of righteousness, for theirs is the kingdom of heaven.

"Blessed are you when people insult you, persecute you and falsely say all kinds of evil against you because of me. Rejoice and be glad, because great is your reward in heaven, for in the same way they persecuted the prophets who were before you."   *Matt. 5:10-12*

Dear friends, do not be surprised at the painful trial you are suffering, as though something strange were happening to you. But rejoice that you participate in the sufferings of Christ, so that you may be overjoyed when his glory is revealed. If you are insulted because of the name of Christ, you are blessed, for the Spirit of glory and of God rests on you.   *1 Peter 4:12-14*

However, if you suffer as a Christian, do not be ashamed, but praise God that you bear that name.   *1 Peter 4:16*

To this you were called, because Christ suffered for you, leaving you an example, that you should follow in his steps. . . . When they hurled their insults at him, he did not retaliate; when he suffered, he made no threats. Instead, he entrusted himself to him who judges justly.
                                              1 Peter 2:21, 23

It is better, if it is God's will, to suffer for doing good than for doing evil. For Christ died for sins once for all, the righteous for the unrighteous, to bring you to God. He was put to death in the body but made alive by the Spirit.
                                              1 Peter 3:17-18

In fact, everyone who wants to live a godly life in Christ Jesus will be persecuted.
                                              2 Tim. 3:12

If we endure, we will also reign with him.
If we disown him, he will also disown us.

2 Tim. 2:12

. . . strengthening the disciples and encouraging them to remain true to the faith. "We must go through many hardships to enter the kingdom of God." . . .

Acts 14:22

His speech persuaded them. They called the apostles in and had them flogged. Then they ordered them not to speak in the name of Jesus, and let them go.

The apostles left the Sanhedrin, rejoicing because they had been counted worthy of suffering disgrace for the Name. Day after day, in the temple courts and from house to house, they never stopped teaching and proclaiming the good news that Jesus is the Christ.

Acts 5:40-42

Therefore, since we are surrounded by such a great cloud of witnesses, let us throw off everything that hinders and the sin that so easily entangles, and let us run with perseverance the race marked out for us. Let us fix our eyes on Jesus, the author and perfecter of our faith, who for the joy set before him endured the cross, scorning its shame, and sat down at the right hand of the throne of God. Consider him who endured such opposition from sinful men, so that you will not grow weary and lose heart.

In your struggle against sin, you have not yet resisted to the point of shedding your blood.

Heb. 12:1-4

"Do not be afraid of what you are about to suffer. I tell you, the devil will put some of you in prison to test you, and you will suffer persecution for ten days. Be faithful, even to the point of death, and I will give you the crown of life."

Rev. 2:10

"Do not be afraid, little flock, for your Father has been pleased to give you the kingdom."

Luke 12:32

8. For Christians who are undergoing trial

And you have forgotten that word of encouragement that addresses you as sons:

"My son, do not make light of the Lord's discipline, and do not lose heart when he rebukes you, because the Lord disciplines those whom he loves, and he punishes everyone he accepts as a son."

Endure hardship as discipline; God is treating you as sons. For what son is not disciplined by his father? . . . No discipline seems pleasant at the time, but painful. Later on, however, it produces a harvest of righteousness and peace for those who have been trained by it. *Heb. 12:5-7, 11*

. . . And into an inheritance that can never perish, spoil or fade—kept in heaven for you, who through faith are shielded by God's power until the coming of the salvation that is ready to be revealed in the last time. In this you greatly rejoice, though now for a little while you may have had to suffer grief in all kinds of trials. These have come so that your faith—of greater worth than gold, which perishes even though refined by fire—may be proved genuine and may result in praise, glory and honour when Jesus Christ is revealed. *1 Peter 1:4-7*

Humble yourselves, therefore, under God's mighty hand, that he may lift you up in due time. Cast all your anxiety on him because he cares for you. *1 Peter 5:6-7*

God is our refuge and strength, an ever present help in trouble.

Therefore we will not fear, though the earth give way and the mountains fall into the heart of the sea, though its waters roar and foam and the mountains quake with their surging. *Ps. 46:1-3*

Even though I walk through the valley of the shadow of death, I will fear no evil, for you are with me; your rod and staff, they comfort me.

Ps. 23:4

A righteous man may have many troubles, but the LORD delivers him from them all;

Ps. 34:19

. . . And call upon me in the day of trouble; I will deliver you, and you will honour me."

Ps. 50:15

The righteous cry out, and the LORD hears them; he delivers them from all their troubles.

Ps. 34:17

The LORD is my light and my salvation—whom shall I fear?

The LORD is the stronghold of my life—of whom shall I be afraid?

When evil men advance against me to devour my flesh, when my enemies and my foes attack me, they will stumble and fall.

Though an army besiege me, my heart will not fear; though war break out against me, even then will I be confident.

One thing I ask of the LORD, this is what I seek: that I may dwell in the house of the LORD all the days of my life, to gaze upon the beauty of the LORD and to seek him in his temple.

For in the day of trouble he will keep me safe in his dwelling; he will hide me in the shelter of his tabernacle and set me high upon a rock.

Then my head will be exalted above the enemies who surround me; at his tabernacle will I sacrifice with shouts of joy; I will sing and make music to the LORD,

I am still confident of this: I will see the goodness of the LORD in the land of the living.

Wait for the LORD; be strong and take heart and wait for the LORD. *Ps. 27:1-6, 13-14*

"Come to me, all you who are weary and burdened, and I will give you rest. Take my yoke upon you and learn from me, for I am gentle and humble in heart, and you will find rest for your souls." *Matt. 11:28-29*

9. For Christians who have lost loved ones

"Do not let your hearts be troubled. Trust in God; trust also in me. In my Father's house are many rooms; if it were not so, I would have told you. I am going there to prepare a place for you. And if I go and prepare a place for you, I will come back and take you to be with me that you also may be where I am. . . .

"Peace I leave with you; my peace I give you. I do not give to you as the world gives. Do not let your hearts be troubled and do not be afraid." *John 14:1-3, 27*

Jesus replied, "You do not realise now what I am doing, but later you will understand." *John 13:7*

"Be still, and know that I am God." *Ps. 46:10*

Then I heard a voice from heaven say, "Write: Blessed are the dead who die in the Lord from now on."

"Yes," says the Spirit, "they will rest from their labour, for their deeds will follow them." *Rev. 14:13*

He answered, "While the child was still alive, I fasted and wept. I thought, 'Who knows? The LORD may be gracious to me and let the child live.' But now that he is dead, why should I fast? Can I bring him back again? I will go to him, but he will not return to me." *2 Sam. 12:22-23*

Brothers, we do not want you to be ignorant about those who fall asleep, or to grieve like the

rest of men, who have no hope. We believe that
Jesus died and rose again and so we believe that
God will bring with Jesus those who have fallen
asleep in him. According to the Lord's own word,
we tell you that we who are still alive, who are left
till the coming of the Lord, will certainly not pre-
cede those who have fallen asleep. For the Lord
himself will come down from heaven, with a loud
command, with the voice of the archangel and
with the trumpet call of God, and the dead in
Christ will rise first. After that, we who are still
alive and are left will be caught up with them in
the clouds to meet the Lord in the air. And so we
will be with the Lord for ever. Therefore encour-
age each other with these words.

1 Thess. 4:13-18

Therefore we are always confident and know
that as long as we are at home in the body we are
away from the Lord. We live by faith, not by
sight, We are confident, I say, and would prefer
to be away from the body and at home with the
Lord. *2 Cor. 5:6-8*

I am torn between the two: I desire to depart
and be with Christ, which is better by far.

Phil. 1:23

So will it be with the resurrection of the dead.
The body that is sown is perishable, it is raised
imperishable; it is sown in dishonour, it is raised
in glory; it is sown in weakness, it is raised in
power; it is sown a natural body, it is raised a
spiritual body. . . . And just as we have borne the
likeness of the earthly man, so shall we bear the
likeness of the man from heaven. . . . For the
perishable must clothe itself with the imperishable, and the mortal with immortality. When the
perishable has been clothed with the imperishable, and the mortal with immortality, then the
saying that is written will come true: "Death has
been swallowed up in victory."

"Where, O death, is your victory? Where, O death, is your sting?"

The sting of death is sin, and the power of sin is the law. But thanks be to God! He gives us the victory through our Lord Jesus Christ.

Therefore, my dear brothers, stand firm. Let nothing move you. Always give yourselves fully to the work of the Lord, because you know that your labour in the Lord is not in vain.

1 Cor. 15:42-44, 49, 53-58